About the Author

Pierre Berton, well-known and well-loved Canadian author,
journalist, and media personality, hailed from Whitehorse, Yukon.
During his career, he wrote fifty books for adults and twenty-two
for children, popularizing Canadian history and culture and
reflecting on his life and times. With more than thirty literary
awards and a dozen honorary degrees to his credit, Berton
was also a Companion of the Order of Canada.

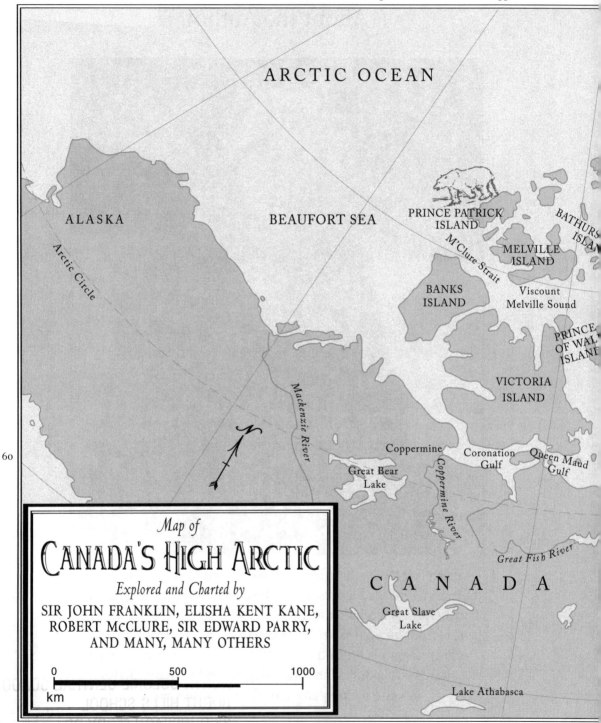

ARCTIC OCEAN

165   135

ALASKA

BEAUFORT SEA

PRINCE PATRICK
ISLAND

BATHURST
ISLAND

M'Clure Strait

MELVILLE
ISLAND

Arctic Circle

BANKS
ISLAND

Viscount
Melville Sound

PRINCE
OF WALES
ISLAND

Mackenzie River

VICTORIA
ISLAND

Coppermine

Coronation
Gulf

Queen Maud
Gulf

60

Great Bear
Lake

Coppermine River

Great Fish River

C A N A D A

Map of

CANADA'S HIGH ARCTIC

Explored and Charted by

SIR JOHN FRANKLIN, ELISHA KENT KANE,
ROBERT McCLURE, SIR EDWARD PARRY,
AND MANY, MANY OTHERS

Great Slave
Lake

0   500   1000

km

Lake Athabasca

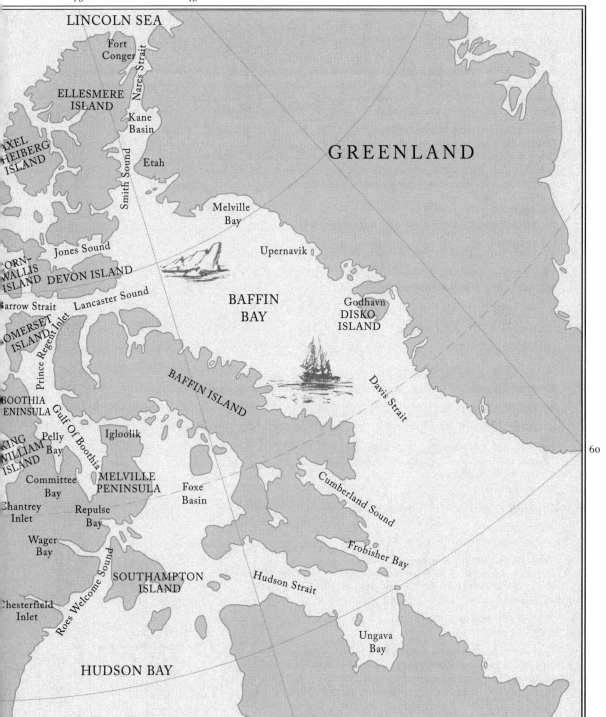

LINCOLN SEA

Fort
Conger

ELLESMERE
ISLAND

Nares Strait

Kane
Basin

GREENLAND

AXEL
HEIBERG
ISLAND

Smith Sound

Etah

Melville
Bay

Jones Sound

Upernavik

CORN-
WALLIS
ISLAND

DEVON ISLAND

Barrow Strait

Lancaster Sound

BAFFIN
BAY

Godhavn
DISKO
ISLAND

SOMERSET
ISLAND

Prince Regent Inlet

BAFFIN ISLAND

Davis Strait

BOOTHIA
PENINSULA

Gulf Of Boothia

Igloolik

KING
WILLIAM
ISLAND

Pelly
Bay

Cumberland Sound

Committee
Bay

MELVILLE
PENINSULA

Foxe
Basin

Chantrey
Inlet

Repulse
Bay

Frobisher Bay

Wager
Bay

Roes Welcome Sound

SOUTHAMPTON
ISLAND

Hudson Strait

Chesterfield
Inlet

Ungava
Bay

HUDSON BAY

Cover and interior design by John Luckhurst
Maps by Brian Smith
Front cover image courtesy Library and Archives Canada, Critical Position of HMS *Investigator* at
    Baring Island, NWT, 1851, C-016105. Back cover image courtesy Library and Archives Canada,
    relics found with the bodies of Franklin's crew, NLC-000734
Copyedited by Joan Tetrault
Proofread by Kirsten Craven
Scans by ABL Imaging

A Note on the Type:
The type in this book is set in Minion, Cloister Open Face and Delphin IIA

The publisher gratefully acknowledges the support of The Canada Council for the Arts
and the Department of Canadian Heritage.

THE CANADA COUNCIL | LE CONSEIL DES ARTS
FOR THE ARTS | DU CANADA
SINCE 1957 | DEPUIS 1957

We acknowledge the financial support of the Government of Canada through the
Book Publishing Industry Development Program (BPIDP) for our publishing activities.

Printed in Canada by Friesens

00 09 08 07 06 / 5 4 3 2 1

First published in the United States in 2006 by
Fitzhenry & Whiteside
121 Harvard Avenue, Suite 2
Allston, MA 02134

Library and Archives Canada Cataloguing in Publication

Berton, Pierre, 1920-2004
    Exploring the frozen North / Pierre Berton.

(Pierre Berton's history for young Canadians)
Collection of 4 previously published works: Parry of the Arctic, Jane Franklin's
obsession, Dr. Kane of the Arctic Seas, and Trapped in the Arctic.
Includes index.

ISBN-13: 978-1-894856-93-5
ISBN-10: 1-894856-93-7

1. Arctic regions--Discovery and exploration--Juvenile literature.
2. Northwest Passage--Discovery and exploration--Juvenile literature.
3. Explorers--Arctic regions--Biography--Juvenile literature. I. Title.
II. Series: Berton, Pierre, 1920- Pierre Berton's history for young Canadians.

G640.B473 2006   j917.95'2041'0922   C2005-907169-9

FIFTH HOUSE LTD.
A Fitzhenry & Whiteside Company
1511, 1800-4 St. SW
Calgary, Alberta T2S 2S5

1-800-387-9776
www.fitzhenry.ca

Exploring the Frozen North
An Omnibus

Pierre Berton

FIFTH
HOUSE

CONTENTS

Foreword *by Eric Wilson*

The Canadian north is a place full of history and adventure. This enchanted land attracts people from around the world.

Pierre Berton is the perfect writer to take you north. His words pull you into the experience—suddenly you are there. You're trudging with Sir John Franklin's men across the frozen lands of King William Island, or setting sail with other rescuers from England in search of his doomed expedition. In its day, the loss of the Franklin expedition was the Really Big Story. Everyone discussed it. Lady Jane Franklin's determination to find her husband and his crew will inspire you. Don't miss this story, or the other northern adventures recounted in these pages. Pierre Berton makes them come alive.

I discovered the north as a young teenager, moving with my family from Vancouver far up the coast to Kitimat. While Kitimat is not at all like King William Island, it was as far north as I had ever been, and it was all new. In those days, the journey to Kitimat was made by coastal steamship. One night I stood alone on the deck. Above, the stars were vivid. Waves rolled away from the hull, but otherwise the night was quiet. Close by, the forest was deeply shadowed. No one lived here—not a light could be seen.

I ached for the city and my friends, but my heart was being captured by something else. From the stern I saw a vast expanse of dark water, glistening with phosphorescence. The moon was low to the ocean, and huge. In the distance were the shapes of mysterious islands. I felt that I was a solitary explorer, discovering a spellbinding place.

I was falling in love with the north.

That feeling has remained with me. I've read everything by Pierre

Berton on northern history. I trust his words to take me there and make it real. But I never appreciated what motivated this man's love of the north until a unique opportunity presented itself. I had the chance to live in Pierre Berton's childhood home as writer in residence.

In August 2004 I journeyed with my wife, Flo, to Dawson City in the Yukon Territory. As a young person, Pierre lived in Dawson with his sister Lucy (who also became an author), and their parents—both clever people themselves. In fact, Laura Berton, Pierre's mother, wrote a book called *I Married the Klondike.* This book was a wonderful discovery for us that summer. It contains gripping, true stories about the people of the Gold Rush and their adventures and heartaches.

Living in Berton House, we shared the family's space. At night we often heard footsteps and assumed that the ghosts of the Bertons were up and about, doing their chores or maybe enjoying a friendly game of chance at the kitchen table. They were probably also around during the daytime! Just like us, they'd have enjoyed the bright flowers and green grass outside. Every day we heard ravens calling to each other with strange liquid notes, the sound clear as crystal in the still, clean air of the north.

Dawson City is a beautiful gem, surrounded by forested mountains. The Yukon River rushes past. Almost daily, Flo and I walked beside it, thinking about the men and women who raced north along this same river in a desperate search for gold. We imagined young Pierre Berton in this setting. Growing up, he listened to the pioneers recall their gold rush adventures. They'd stayed in the north, loving the place. Perhaps, we speculated, those oldtimers inspired young Pierre's decision to write about our nation's history.

It's easy to understand why Pierre Berton loved the north. You only have to hear the people speak of the winters with such passion. Flo and I heard them recount tales of dog sledding under the vivid lights that dance across the night skies, sleeping burrowed down in the snow, or about spending winters alone in a cabin, far away down the river, as far as possible from human contact, alone except for an easel and some paints and the inspiration of the frozen land all around.

Writers have always gathered such stories, and many have lived in the north. Pierre Berton was surely inspired by his own neighbour, a poet named Robert Service—his cabin is just across the gravel road from the Berton's home. Robert Service has motivated many writers; his story is legendary. As a young man he worked at a bank in Dawson City, but one day he quit! He gave it up and became a full-time writer. Now that's enough to inspire dreams in a youngster like Pierre Berton, but wait, there's more. Robert Service didn't just become a writer, he became a hugely successful writer. He was world famous—everyone read his wonderful poems, including kings and queens. But here's what really encouraged Pierre Berton— Robert Service didn't become successful by writing about faraway places with strange-sounding names. Instead, he told stories about the Klondike and the days of the gold rush. People all over the world loved his work, and yet he wrote about Dawson City and the Yukon.

Flo and I pictured young Pierre on summer days, sitting on the porch steps, gazing at the poet's cabin. If success could happen to Robert Service, it could happen to Pierre Berton. How often did he make such a vow, we wondered, and how grand were the young man's dreams?

Well, positive thinking worked for Pierre. As an author, he published many successful books. As a personality, he dominated the early years of Canadian television. Pierre Berton was an adventurer and a loving family man, giving and kind. It was his own generosity that made Berton House possible. He purchased the building, and paid for renovations. Because of this, other writers can sit on the steps of Berton House, gazing across the street at Robert Service's cabin. They, too, can be inspired by the success of Robert Service—and the Bertons.

Many Canadians credit Pierre Berton with giving us a love of our history. He gathered wonderful tales about our past, and told them in such a way that we can understand and appreciate the people who, over the years, have been part of Canada. Many of their stories are here in these pages.

Now, faithful reader, please turn to the words of Pierre Berton himself and be prepared for adventure!

Eric Wilson
www.ericwilson.com

First communication with the Natives of Prince Regent's Bay,
as drawn by John Sacheuse and presented to Captain Ross,
August 10, 1818. John Sacheuse was the John Ross 1818
Expedition's Inuit interpreter, a Native North American.

(COURTESY LIBRARY AND ARCHIVES CANADA, C-025238)

PARRY OF THE ARCTIC

CONTENTS

CHAPTER ONE

The Strange People

WHEN EDWARD PARRY WAS JUST THIRTEEN YEARS OLD, HE LEFT GRAMMAR SCHOOL IN ENGLAND AND JOINED THE ROYAL NAVY AS A YOUNG MIDSHIPMAN. THAT WAS THE AMBITION OF MANY YOUNG ENGLISH BOYS—AN AMBITION THAT COULD BE FULFILLED IF YOU KNEW THE RIGHT PEOPLE AND WERE BRIGHT ENOUGH TO BE ACCEPTED INTO THE SERVICE. MIDSHIPMEN WERE NAVAL APPRENTICES. MOST WHO JOINED AT THE AGE OF THIRTEEN WOULD RISE TO BECOME OFFICERS IN THE NAVY, AND MANY WOULD BECOME ADMIRALS. PARRY BECAME ONE OF THE GREATEST EXPLORERS OF HIS ERA.

That was, of course, the ambition of many young men in the nineteenth century. Explorers were the great heroes of the era—an era that has been called "The Golden Age of Exploration." To unravel the secret of the source of the Nile, to enter into darkest Africa, to explore the unknown islands of the South Seas, or to face the mists of the Arctic in a search for the fabulous North West Passage—these were the goals that they sought.

Explorers were as wildly popular then as movie stars or rock stars or television stars are today. They were knighted by the queen. They wrote best-selling books and articles. They were given huge sums of money as prizes. They were pursued in the streets by fans. They were courted by women who wanted them at their society tables. Their lectures were attended by thousands. In short, they were as famous as the prime minister himself.

Parry was just twenty-eight years old when the Royal Navy put him in charge of a ship—one of two that would try to search out the North West Passage. In those days the Canadian Arctic was an unknown quantity. No one knew what existed at the top of the North American continent. One man, Alexander Mackenzie, had actually reached the Arctic Ocean in 1789 when he came down the river that bears his name to its mouth. Another,

Samuel Hearne, had reached the mouth of the Coppermine in 1771. Apart from these two pinpoints on the map, nobody knew anything about the Arctic coast that was supposed to form the northern roof of the continent—indeed, nobody was quite sure whether there *was* an Arctic coast. Hudson Bay had been partially explored and men had reached the tip of Baffin Island. But what lay beyond and to the west? Was it open ocean? Was it solid land? Was it a whole tangle of islands and channels? And was there a passage that would link the two great oceans, the Atlantic with the Pacific?

The wars with Napoleon ended in 1815. Because the Navy had nothing for its young men to do, it set about to explore the oceans of the world—including the Arctic. Three years after the end of the Napoleonic wars, the Navy sent two ships into that frozen Arctic world. The lead ship was the *Isabella*, captained by an old naval hand named John Ross. The smaller ship, the *Alexander*, was placed under the charge of Edward Parry.

Here were cathedrals and palaces, statues and castles, all brilliant white, flashing in the sun's rays, each slightly blurred as in a dream —a world of shimmering ice.

In mid-June, 1818, the expedition had crossed the Atlantic and entered Davis Strait between Baffin Island and Greenland. The officers and crews now had their first view of the icebound sea in all its splendour and all its menace. Here was a brilliant world of blue, emerald, and white—dazzling to the eye. To some, the great frozen mountains—icebergs—that whirled past seemed to have been carved by some mysterious artist. Here were cathedrals and palaces, statues and castles, all brilliant white, flashing in the sun's rays, each slightly blurred as in a dream—a world of shimmering ice. Colours were intense. As Parry's superior, Ross, wrote: "They glitter with a vividness of colour beyond the power of art to represent."

Both men were awed by the strangeness of the savage realm they had entered. Soon they would be in unknown waters. But it was comforting to encounter the fleet of three dozen whaling ships, all flying the British flag, and to hear the cheers of the whalers as they passed through. This was where civilization ended.

The whalers gave Parry and Ross the first warning about the difficulties of the Arctic climate, which changed from year to year. This year the ice was much worse than expected. The previous winter had been the worst in ten years. The whalers could hardly find a clear passage south through the ocean of icebergs.

On July 1, the two ships entered a frightening maze of ice. Parry tried to count the icebergs and gave up when he reached a thousand. For the next month the two ships worked their way north along the Greenland coast, blinded by fog and almost crushed by the pressure of the ice pack, that vast floating ocean of solid ice, during one terrible gale. It was a close call: the sterns of the two vessels bashed into each other. Spars, rigging, life boats were torn apart. But they survived.

A day or so later, at the very western tip of Greenland, they came face-to-face with an unknown culture. These were the Inuit, whom they then called Eskimo. Even John Sacheuse, their Native interpreter from South Greenland, had never heard of this strange race of polar people, whom Ross named "Arctic Highlanders." Sacheuse could understand their dialect only with great difficulty.

A picture of this first encounter between white men and Inuit people appears at the beginning of this book. Notice that the Inuit are dressed as one might expect, in clothes made from fur and sealskin—perfect for the Arctic climate. But the two men who greet them—Ross and Parry—are dressed exactly as they would have been if they'd gone to the South Seas. They wore their cocked hats, tail coats, white gloves, and swords, as if they were attending a party in London. The fact was, of course, that no exploring nation had yet understood the need for special clothing in the North.

If the British officers were baffled by these people muffled in furs, the Natives were equally baffled. "Where do you come from, the sun or the moon?" they asked. And so the picture was made, not by the British, but by Sacheuse himself. He was a young Christianized Native from the South who had stowed away two years before on a sailing ship and eventually reached England where he studied drawing. He was the first Arctic Native encountered by British explorers.

A very strange and almost comic scene followed. The Inuit hung back, terrified of the strange people on the ships. And so it was decided that one of Parry's officers would go out with a white flag on which was painted the white man's emblem of peace—a hand holding an olive branch.

The only trouble was, the Natives didn't know what an olive branch was or what it was supposed to mean. No olive trees grew on that bleak shore. In fact, no trees grew at all. Yet none of the white men seemed to think this strange. Ross, however, was more practical. He put a flag on a pole and tied a bag full of presents to it and that worked very well.

These strange people had had no contact with the world beyond their own region. They were surprised at the presence of Sacheuse. It hadn't occurred to them that there might be others like themselves in the world. As for the men with the white skins, they thought they had come from the sky.

These were landsmen. They didn't know anything about boats. They had never even seen a boat. Even the Native word "kayak" had no meaning for them. They spoke to the ships as if they were living things. "We have seen them move their wings," they said. Sacheuse tried to explain the ships were floating houses. They had trouble believing him.

They were baffled by their first glimpse into a mirror and tried to discover the monster they believed was hiding behind it. They laughed at the metal frames of the eye-glasses worn by some of the sailors. When they were offered a biscuit, they spat it out in disgust. They wondered what kind of ice the window panes were made of. They tried to figure what kind of animals produced the strange "skins" the officers were wearing. When they were shown a watch, they thought it was alive and asked if it was good to eat. The sight of a little pig terrified them. A demonstration of hammer and nails charmed them. The ship's furniture baffled them, for the only wood they'd ever seen came from a tiny shrub, whose stem was no thicker than a finger.

Sacheuse made them take off their caps in the presence of the officers. That suggests how quickly he had absorbed the white way of life. It was the first attempt—one of many that would be made over the coming years—to "civilize" the Natives.

They obeyed cheerfully enough. But they must have been as mystified by this ritual as the English were to find that human beings actually lived in this strange and cruel land. Yet nobody asked how it was that this band of people had managed to adapt to the savage wilderness of Greenland. If they had done so, it would have been easier in the future for British sailors to adapt to the Arctic way of life.

The expedition moved on to the very top of Baffin Bay and then sailed west to the southern tip of what is now Ellesmere Island. It turned south still seeking a channel that might lead to the North West Passage.

Then, at the end of August, they encountered a long inlet leading westward, which an earlier explorer had named for Sir James Lancaster. Was this the way to the Orient? Or was it simply a dead end? Nobody knew.

Parry was full of optimism. He was sure this was the route that would lead, if not to the Russian coast, at least into the heart of the Arctic to connect with other lanes of water to the west.

Ross wasn't so sure. As the two ships moved into the unknown, he became convinced that no passage existed. Then, one foggy afternoon at the end of August they reached the thirty-mile (48-km) point, and Ross pulled up, waiting for Parry to catch him and for the weather to clear. The officer of the watch roused him in his cabin to announce the fog was lifting. And this is where Ross made the blunder that wrecked his career and paved the way for Edward Parry to achieve greatness.

Parry was full of optimism. He was sure this was the route that would lead, if not to the Russian coast, at least into the heart of the Arctic to connect with other lanes of water to the west.

Ross saw, or thought he saw, a chain of mountains blocking all access to the west. Nobody else saw it. Was it an Arctic mirage that baffled Ross? These would become well known in the years that followed. Or was Ross seeking an excuse to end the journey, as many believed? To the stunned surprise and anger of the others, Ross, without a word of explanation, turned about and headed for home "as if some mischief was behind him."

As William Hooper, the purser of Parry's ship, wrote, "Thus vanished our golden dreams, our brilliant hopes, our high expectations!" Parry and his crew were bitterly disappointed. They had expected to spend a year in the Arctic, and now here was Ross hightailing it back for England.

The Navy was not amused. They sided with Parry, retired Ross on half pay, and never used him again. The following year they sent Parry off at the head of an expedition to find the North West Passage.

Actually, Parry was no better qualified for Arctic exploration than the unhappy John Ross. Parry owed his position to John Barrow, Jr., the moon-faced bureaucrat who was the unseen power behind the British Navy. Barrow, the civil servant—he was actually *second* secretary to the Admiralty, though he acted as if he were the first—has been called the father of modern Arctic exploration. It was he who sent ship after ship around the world charting unknown waters off the coasts of Africa and Asia. But it was the Arctic that obsessed him.

He held the curious belief that somewhere beyond the impenetrable ice, there lay a warmer ocean, surrounding the North Pole but walled off from the world by a frozen barrier. He was dead wrong—how could you have warm water surrounded by a doughnut-shaped circle of ice? Yet Barrow's belief in an "Open Polar Sea," as he called it, persisted for half a century.

One man who knew that was nonsense was a whaling captain, William Scoresby, the most courageous and skillful skipper in the Greenland fleet. He was more than that; a student of philosophy and science, and an inventor, he was the leading expert on Arctic conditions, and was about to complete a monumental work on the subject.

He would have been a better choice than Parry to lead the first exploration into the Arctic puzzle. But it was Parry, the regular naval man, who got the nod from the powerful John Barrow. Barrow was positively chilly, if not rude, when Scoresby approached him, suggesting he be allowed on the expedition.

In its arrogance, the Navy scorned whalers. Under the rigid English class system, they weren't "gentlemen." Neither was Barrow, who came from humble stock, or even Parry, though his father, a doctor, had members of nobility as patients.

But the Navy was convinced its own officers and men were capable of anything. Had Nelson not defeated the French at Trafalgar? Besides, Parry had powerful friends and, in the Royal Navy of 1818, it was who you knew, not what you knew, that counted.

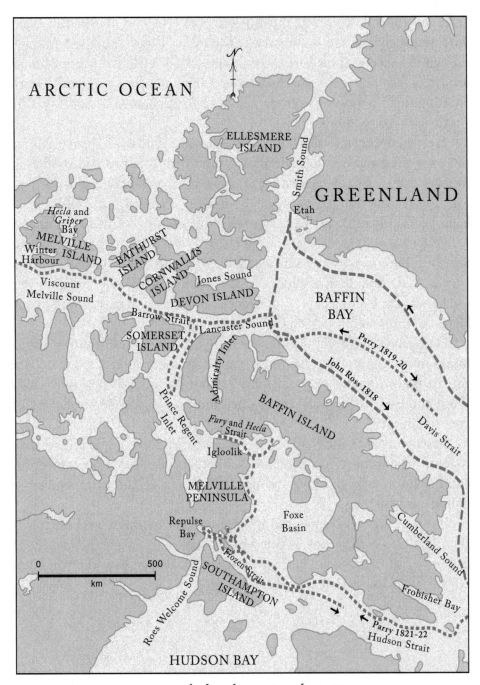

Voyages of Edward Parry into the Arctic

CHAPTER TWO

Into the Unknown

EDWARD PARRY BELONGED TO A NEW GENERATION OF EXPLORERS. HE WAS THE MODEL BY WHICH THOSE WHO FOLLOWED WOULD BE JUDGED. HE BELIEVED THAT AN ENGLISHMAN COULD OVERCOME ANY OBSTACLE. DEVOUT, STEADFAST, AND LOYAL, HE BELIEVED IN HARD WORK AND TEAM SPIRIT.

A handsome officer, tall, slightly stooped, with curly chestnut hair and soft grey eyes, he was well-spoken and eager to please. He was not an excitable man. His journals did not make too much of the hardships he faced. But he was lucky. He sailed north at the right moment, when the Arctic channels were clearer of ice than they had been in a decade.

But his real achievement lay not in opening a passage to the Arctic islands. His greatest accomplishment was his understanding of his crew and his determination to keep them healthy in mind as well as body.

These were tiny ships by our standards. You could set both of them down, end to end, in a modern football field and still have some room left over. Being ships of war, they were made for the open sea, not the shallow coastal waters of the Arctic maze. Crammed together in these close quarters, sleeping in hammocks, buffeted by mountainous waves and shrieking gales, unable to leave their vessels during the long Arctic night, each seaman's good nature was tested and often found wanting. The food was dreadful—mainly salt pork—while the beer, which was their main beverage, grew stale and sour after months in barrels. Their confinement was as prison-like as that suffered by modern astronauts, but unlike these twentieth-century explorers, they had no support system, no information network, no form of electronic monitoring. They were on their own—out of touch with the world for months and usually for years. Yet they survived, and this was Parry's achievement.

Parry realized that the greatest peril of wintering in the Arctic would not be the cold. It would be boredom. For as long as ten months nothing moved. The ships became prisons. The masts and superstructure had to be taken down. The hatches were hermetically sealed. The ships were smothered in blankets of insulating snow.

Given the cramped conditions, the best disciplined seaman could break down. Small irritations could be magnified into raging quarrels. Imagined insults could lead to mutinous talk and even mutiny. Parry was determined to cope with the monotony of the Arctic winter. All the officers under him were young men—for the Arctic required youth, energy, and physical fitness. Parry and his crew had these qualities.

By April 1819, the two ships in their fresh coating of black and yellow paint were ready to set off. Down at the docks at Greenwich the well-wishers flocked. Parry wrote that "no other expedition had ever attracted a more hearty feeling of national interest." One of the visitors particularly attracted him—a Miss Browne, who was the niece of one of his officers. They flirted together. Perhaps Parry thought that when he returned he would marry her.

The ships left on May 11, heading across the Atlantic. Parry's instruction was to head directly up Davis Strait to Lancaster Sound—the same opening in the wall of mountains that had fooled John Ross. If it turned out that there *were* mountains, as Ross had thought, Parry was ordered to go on north and find another entry into the Arctic world.

His task was to get right through as quickly as possible, deliver his documents to the Russian governor at Kamchatka, and then sail on to Hawaii and return home. His superiors were overly optimistic about the Arctic. They believed Parry could get through perhaps in one year and certainly in two. But Parry thought that the possibility of getting into China that year was "too much to hope for." Too much indeed! Almost ninety years would pass before anybody made it.

Parry's chances of bulling his way through were slimmer than he knew. In a bad season the odds were about one in a hundred, in a light season, about fifty-fifty. Even in an exceptional season—and this *was* an exceptional season—there was still a 25 percent chance of failure.

Parry's first setback came when he ran into the great river of ice that breaks off from the polar pack and pours down the centre of Davis Strait. The ice pack was impenetrable—a vast ocean of icebergs all frozen together. Dozens of feet deep, it stretched off to the horizon as far as the eye could see—a great, rumpled sheet of white that even today can resist a modern icebreaker. Nonetheless Parry decided boldly to try to force his way directly through. That shortcut would save weeks. He would use his larger ship, *Hecla*, as a battering ram to clear the way for the weaker ship, *Griper*.

That didn't work. Unable to get through the barrier, he turned north for three weeks and crossed the Arctic Circle into Baffin Bay. There he tried again to bull his way through by brute force.

His crews experienced for the first time the exhausting toil that would be a feature of Arctic exploration for all of the nineteenth century. They had to sit in small boats, straining at the oars, as they attempted to tow the big vessels through the ice-choked channels. They attached cables to anchors in the icebergs and pulled the ships westward, foot by foot. They trudged along the ice floes, clinging to ropes like tug-of-war teams, hauling the vessels in the direction of their goal.

It was disappointing work. On one long day they sweated for eleven hours and moved no more than four miles (6.4 km). Once, when the *Hecla* was trapped, they worked for seven hours with ice saws to cut her free, only to find her frozen in again at the end of the day. Parry urged them on with extra rations of rum and meat. In the distance they could hear the music of the great black whales, a shrill ringing sound, rather like hundreds of musical glasses badly played.

At last they were through. The broad entrance to Lancaster Sound lay directly ahead. The towering mountains of Bylot Island crowned its southern entrance. Now Parry knew that the next few days would either make his reputation or break it. He couldn't wait for the slower ship, *Griper*. On August 1, as soon as the wind was favourable, he set out himself up the sound under full sail.

The weather was clear. The mysterious channel lay open. As the wind increased to a gale, Parry could sense that everyone on the ship was holding his breath. Nobody had sailed up this lane of water since the days of the Iceland fishermen six centuries before. Everything was new. Long inlets— or were they only bays?—led into the unknown from both shores. Broken hills in the south rose one above the other to snow-clad peaks. Was there land ahead? Was the route to the Passage blocked as Ross had believed? No one knew.

But the lookout, high up in the crow's nest—a barrel tied to the top mast—could find no hint of any mountains. The sound—eighty miles (129 km) wide—appeared to be clear of ice. For two days the ship moved on. Now all hands began to feel a sense of relief. There were some who began to believe the Passage could be mastered.

At six o'clock on the evening of August 4, their hopes were dashed. The lookout reported land ahead and everybody's spirits fell. But then, the land turned out to be a small island, and it was now obvious that the channel ahead was clear. John Ross's failing eyesight had played him false. Parry, who had never believed in these mysterious mountains, felt vindicated.

Parry's smaller ship, the *Griper*, joined him here. Parry's purser, William Hooper, wrote that "there was something peculiarly animating in the joy which lighted every countenance … we've arrived in a sea which had never before been navigated, we were gazing on land that European eyes had never before beheld … and before us was the prospect of realizing all our wishes and exalting the honour of our country …"

Parry could now see that a water highway stretched straight as an arrow directly into the heart of the unknown Arctic islands. But he was groping with the unknown. He was like a man travelling through a long tunnel, able only to guess at the mysteries that lay to the north and south.

He could see precipices on the north shore, cut by chasms and fjords, some of them rising for five hundred feet (152 m). On the south he could see a tableland, cut by broad channels, one of them more than forty miles (64 km) wide. But was this the route to the Bering Sea and the Pacific Ocean? He had no way of knowing.

Blocked by ice ahead of him, he turned south into a new channel forty miles (64 km) wide which he named Prince Regent Inlet. The two ships sailed down it for more than a hundred miles (160 km) past the snow-choked ravines and high rock walls of a great island (Somerset). There, more ice barred his way.

Now he faced a new dilemma. Perhaps this was only a bay after all! And so he turned about and sailed back to Lancaster Sound. He found some open water along the north shore but was held up again by snow and sleet.

Finally the weather cleared and he headed west into the very heart of the mysterious Arctic.

He left the high cliffs and peaks above the coastline of Devon Island and plunged into the northern mists of a broad channel, which he named for the Duke of Wellington. He swept on, past the rock walls of Cornwallis Island and the wriggling fjords of Bathurst Island. Finally, he entered an immense inland sea that he named Viscount Melville Sound after the first lord of the Admiralty.

Parry and his crew had been promised a five-thousand-pound reward by Parliament if they could cross the meridian at 110°. On Sunday, September 4, they did it. For his feat Parry would be given a thousand pounds—a small fortune at that time, worth more than $100,000 today.

It was well earned. In one remarkable five-week sweep he had explored some eight hundred miles (1,287 km) of new coastline. And there was more: to the north he could see the twelve-hundred-foot (366-m) cliffs and rugged highlands of another great island, which he also named for Viscount Melville.

Eighteen days later, with the weather getting worse and more ice forming, he gave up the struggle. This was as far as he could go that year. He would have to go into winter quarters in a small bay on Melville Island's south shore. That would be his prison for the best part of a year.

Now the back-breaking work began. The crew laboured for nineteen hours without a break in the ghostly glimmer of the northern lights, sawing a channel, square by square, in the bay ice. Every time they cut it open it seemed to refreeze before their eyes. But after three days they had managed to cut an opening two and a third miles (3.7 km) long into the bay. There the ships would rest for more than eight months protected from the fury of the sea by a reef of rocks. Parry named it Winter Harbour.

Now these Englishmen were marooned at the very heart of the darkest and most desolate realm in all the northern hemisphere. The nearest permanent civilized community lay twelve hundred miles (1,930 km) to the east on an island off Greenland's west coast. The nearest white men were the fur traders on Great Slave Lake, seven hundred miles (1,127 km) to the south. Another twelve hundred miles (1,930 km) to the southwest were the uninhabited shores of Russian Alaska, and beyond that, Siberia. To the north, a frozen world stretched, stark and empty, to the Pole.

Thus for hundreds of miles in every direction the land was devoid of human life. The nearest Inuit were close to five hundred miles (800 km) away. Soon the wildlife itself would vanish. New species that they had seen—muskoxen, caribou, and lemmings—would be gone, and so would the gulls and the terns. The only light they would have would be the flickering candles, rationed carefully to one inch (2.5 cm) a day. For the sun itself would depart with the animals.

These were the first white men to winter in the Arctic. Under such conditions Parry knew that men could become half-crazed. His purpose was to keep his crew so busy that they wouldn't have time to brood. There would be plenty of daily exercise, regular inspections, and afternoons crammed with work, much of which Parry would invent. The emphasis was on physical health, cleanliness, and "busyness."

At 5:45 in the morning the men were up scrubbing the decks with warm sand. They had breakfast at eight, were inspected right down to their fingernails at 9:15, and then set about running around the deck or, in good weather, on the shore. They were kept occupied all afternoon, drawing, knitting yarn, or making gaskets. After supper they were allowed to play games or sing and dance until bedtime at nine. The officers spent a quieter evening. They read books, wrote letters, and played chess or musical instruments.

Around them in the gathering gloom, the land stretched off, desolate and dreary, deathlike in its stillness, offering no interest for the eye or amusement for the mind. Parry noted that if he spotted a stone of more than usual size on one of the short walks he took from the ship, his eyes were drawn to it and he found himself pulled in its direction. So deceptive was the unchanging surface of the snow that objects apparently half a mile (800 m) away could be reached after a minute's walk.

In such a landscape it was easy for a man to get lost. As a result, Parry forbade anyone to wander from the ships. And when darkness fell, their isolation was complete. In mid-season one could, with great difficulty, read a newspaper by daylight—but only at noon.

He had no idea how cold it could be in the Arctic. He found that the slightest touch of a bare hand on a metal object tore off the skin. A telescope placed against his eye burned like a red-hot brand. Leather boots were totally impractical because they froze hard and brought on frostbite. Parry devised a more flexible footwear of canvas and green hide.

Sores wouldn't heal. Lemon juice and vinegar froze solid and broke their containers. The very mercury froze in the thermometers. When doors were opened, a thick fog poured down the hatchways, condensing on the walls and turning to ice.

Damp bedding froze, forcing the men into hammocks. Even the steam rising from the bake ovens froze—which meant that there was less bread to eat. And there wasn't enough fuel to heat the ships. The crews were always cold. The officers played chess bundled up in scarves and greatcoats.

> *He found that the slightest touch of a bare hand on a metal object tore off the skin. A telescope placed against his eye burned like a red-hot brand.*

Nevertheless, the expedition produced and printed a weekly newspaper to which Parry himself contributed. They put on plays and skits, the female impersonators shivering gamely in their thin garments. Parry admitted it was almost too cold for the actors and the audience to enjoy the shows. No wonder! In his own cabin the temperature dropped in February to just seven degrees Fahrenheit (-14° C).

By mid-March, twenty men were sick and Parry began to look ahead. When would the thaw come? How long must they remain in prison? It was still bitingly cold a month later. Parry hadn't figured on that. He now began to have some doubts about getting through to the west.

Two weeks dragged by. The sun now shone at midnight. The temperature moved back to the freezing point. Game began to appear—a few ptarmigan and, a month later, caribou. The fresh meat reduced the danger of scurvy, although one man died from it at the end of June.

Parry decided on a two-week trip across the big island. He took four officers and eight men. They dragged eight hundred pounds (363 kg) of equipment on a two-wheeled cart. Strangely, it didn't occur to them to use dogs and sledges as the Inuit did.

Then July arrived. That was the only bearable month on the island. Yet ice still choked the harbour. Parry was desperate to be off. His sails were ready for an immediate start. He realized how little time he had—nine weeks at the most—a painful truth he couldn't hide from the crew.

The days that followed in late July and early August were maddening. The ice melted. They moved forward. The ice blocked their way. They anchored. The ice shifted. They moved again. The wind changed. The ice moved back.

On August 4, they were able at last to set off into the west, but again the ice stopped them. The floes closed in on the *Griper* hoisting her two feet (0.6 m) out of the water.

Parry sent an officer ashore to climb a high cliff and look over the frozen sea to the west. He reported land fifty miles (80 km) away, but the sea itself was covered with ice floes as far as the eye could reach. They were so closely joined that no gleam of water shone through. Parry named the new land Banks Island after the president of the Royal Society, but he did not reach it.

Now his optimism began to fade. The previous summer the Passage had seemed within his grasp. All winter he had planned to break out of the harbour and to sail on to the Bering Sea, but now the Arctic was showing its real face.

The ice kept him in prison for five more days. When it cleared he tried to go northwest. Again the ice stopped him. He ran east looking for a southern way out, but once more found himself frozen in. Like a rat in a trap, he was scurrying this way and that, trying to escape.

On August 23, he managed to reach Cape Providence on the southern tip of Melville Island after performing "six miles (9.6 km) of the most difficult navigation I have ever known among ice." He couldn't know then that he was facing the dreaded ice stream that flows down from the Beaufort Sea where the ice is fifty feet (15.2 m) thick. The polar pack squeezing down past Banks Island into Melville Sound and on to the channels that lead south and east to the North American coast is all but impassable. One hundred and twenty-four years would pass before the motor of the tough little RCMP schooner, *St. Roch*, would finally push it through the barrier on the eastern side of the present Banks Island.

Parry was heartsick. Now he had to admit that he couldn't do it. It wouldn't have given him much comfort if he had known the truth—that no sailing vessel would ever conquer the Passage, and no other vessel either, in his century. He had gone as far as any man could go in the primitive conditions of that time.

He had a decision to make. He knew he could stretch his food and fuel for another winter by careful rationing. But he couldn't answer for his crews' health. And so he turned his ships east, hoping to find an alternate passage to the south. None appeared. At the end of August he set off for England and was home by the end of October, with all but one of the ninety-four men who had gone north with him.

He'd been deceived by the vagaries of Arctic weather. He hadn't reckoned on the severity of the climate, or the shortness of the season. He was convinced, quite rightly, that his chosen route was impossible. If the Passage was to be conquered, another way must be found.

Still, he remained an optimist. Promoted to commander, cheered up by the applause of the politicians, the congratulations of the Navy, and the cheers of the public, he could be pardoned for believing that the next time he would make it. But almost nine decades would pass before any white explorer travelled from the Atlantic to the Pacific by way of the cold Arctic seas.

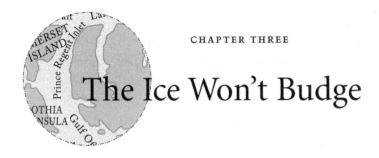

CHAPTER THREE

The Ice Won't Budge

PARRY BECAME THE NINETEENTH CENTURY'S FIRST HERO EXPLORER. THESE WERE FOLK FIGURES LARGER THAN LIFE. THEIR FAILINGS, FLAWS, AND HUMAN WEAKNESSES WERE IGNORED BY THE PUBLIC AND THE PRESS, WHO SAW THEM AS LEADERS IN A GROWING BRITISH EMPIRE.

Fortune accompanied fame. Parry had his thousand pounds from Parliament—an enormous sum in those days. Now he got another thousand from a British publisher for the rights to his journal. Letters of congratulations poured in. He might not have discovered the Passage, but he had, in his phrase, "made a large hole in it."

His time was occupied by a round of social events that might have turned the head of a more excitable officer. His portrait was painted by a member of the Royal Academy. He was given the freedom of his native city, Bath. He was presented at court. The new king, George IV, offered congratulations. London hostesses scrambled to invite him to dinner. Exclusive clubs asked him to become a member. The first of the Arctic heroes was setting a pattern that others would seek to copy. Considering the rewards, who would not dare to brave the Arctic blasts?

And certainly Parry was eager to be off again. That winter of 1820-21, he began to prepare for his second voyage to conquer the Passage. Indeed, Parry felt he was in a race. His main fear was that the Russians would beat the English to it.

Before the year was out, the decision was made. Again there would be two ships, the *Hecla*, and a new ship, the *Fury*, which was the *Hecla*'s sister. Parry would command the *Fury*. The *Hecla*'s commander would be a dashing young lieutenant, George Lyon, who was used to hardship. He'd barely survived a mission to the desert interior of North Africa in which a companion had died.

Parry was determined to keep his men occupied and entertained. This time trunks of theatrical costumes were packed aboard, along with a printing press, a magic lantern that could project coloured pictures on a bed-sheet screen, and a full supply of library books. Parry decided to establish a school during the long Arctic nights to teach his crew to learn to read their bibles.

He expected to spend at least two winters in the Arctic and he piled provisions for three winters on board his ships just in case he had to spend a third. To help stop scurvy, he proposed to grow great quantities of mustard and cress, and he ordered stacks of hot frames for that purpose. Fresh vegetables were known to ward off the disease.

He would fight off the cold and the dampness with a newly designed "Sylvester Stove" that would carry warm air to every part of the hermetically sealed ship. Because there would be lots of fuel this time, it would burn day and night. He also improvised new footwear—using canvas tops and insulated cork soles—and he supplied deerskin jackets for his men.

"Oh, how I long to be among the ice!" exclaimed Parry with all the zest of a schoolboy. His route would be different this time. The only other known avenue leading into the Arctic was the original route taken by Henry Hudson, way back in 1610. It was just possible that a passage might be found leading westward out of Hudson Bay.

The most likely opening was Repulse Bay, which had repulsed other explorers in the previous century. Still, it had only been partially explored. Was it really a bay? Perhaps like Lancaster Sound it might be a strait. That was Parry's initial goal.

Once again at Deptford the crowds swarmed aboard Parry's ship, *Hecla*, to walk the decks and touch the railings that had once been encased in ice, and to bask in the ordeal. Parry organized a grand ball aboard the sister ship *Fury*, which was decked out for the occasion. As the band played on the upper deck, the company danced on and on into the night under a rising moon, each man and woman convinced he or she was in the presence of adventure.

Ten days later—April 27, 1821—both vessels were ready to sail. When they reached Hudson Strait, Parry sent a final letter home. He wrote, "I never felt so strongly the vanity, uncertainty, and comparative unimportance of everything this world can give, and the paramount necessity of preparation for another and a better life than this." The Arctic had made him humble.

The only known way to reach Repulse Bay was to circle around the western shores of Southampton Island at the very top of Hudson Bay. Parry, however, decided to gamble by taking a shortcut through the mysterious Frozen Strait, which lay to the northeast.

That was unknown territory. Some didn't believe the strait existed. Half the available maps didn't even show it. Parry wasn't even sure that he had reached the entrance to it, and so plunged blindly on in a thick fog and fierce blizzard. Then he found to his surprise that he actually got through the strait without knowing it. And it wasn't frozen at all.

He had hoped Repulse Bay would be the link to the Arctic. Now he found that it was landlocked, a dead end. This was not the route to the Passage. If one was to be found, it must be farther north.

For the next six weeks Parry searched for a way out. But he could find no promising inlet that would lead westward. On October 8, he gave up. He found an anchorage on the east coast of Melville Peninsula (also named for the first lord) and anchored at a point he called Winter Island. And there once again he was imprisoned by the ice until the following July.

The long winter passed more comfortably than the one Parry had endured on the earlier voyage. The new stove worked well. Scurvy was not a problem because of the mustard and cress that he managed to grow. Nor was the crew affected by the melancholy brought on by the long nights, because Parry's wintering place was much farther south and the sun didn't completely vanish.

And there were diversions. The officers shaved off their whiskers to play female roles in the theatre. The school was a great success. By year's end, every man had learned to read. But the greatest event was the arrival on February 1 of a band of sixty Inuit. As Parry wrote, "they were as desirous of pleasing us as we were ready to be pleased." Soon there was singing and dancing on the decks as the newcomers made repeated visits to the ships. The presence of these strangers made much of the winter bearable. As Parry noted, the Natives "served in no small degree to enliven us at this season."

Still the North West Passage continued to elude him. He sent Lyon off on a fortnight's sledge trip up the Melville Peninsula to seek an opening to the west—a journey that left all the travellers badly frostbitten. Lyon couldn't find the Passage, though he thought there might be a route around the peninsula to the north.

Desperate to get his ships free of ice, Parry kept his crews toiling for three weeks to saw a channel out to open water. Two men died, perhaps from the effects of the work. But on July 2 he was able to set his course north.

He reached a Native village, Igloolik, at the top of Foxe Basin. And there he encountered another barrier. Fortunately the Inuit turned out to be expert map-makers. Their simple charts convinced Parry that a passage existed to the west.

Once again he sent Lyon across the ice with a band of Inuit to pick up fresh fish and to assess the chances of getting through. Lyon enjoyed living with the Natives. He learned to eat their food. He danced with the Native women and taught them to play leapfrog. He even allowed himself to be tattooed in the Native style.

> *Fortunately the Inuit turned out to be expert map-makers. Their simple charts convinced Parry that a passage existed to the west.*

But he found no open water. The ice was still as thick as three feet (1 m) with the land obscured by fog. Parry's patience was wearing thin. He was convinced he was at the threshold of the Passage, but he couldn't move.

The Inuit maps had indicated the presence of a narrow fjord. Did that actually lead to the open sea? Parry decided to find out for himself. On August 18, 1822, he stood on the north point of the Melville Peninsula overlooking the narrowest part of the inlet the Inuit had shown. Toward the west where the water widened, he could see no land. He was certain he had discovered the polar sea, and he was convinced that he could force his way by this narrow strait into the west. All he had to do was wait for the ice to clear.

But the ice did not clear. The weather grew warm. An eastern breeze sprang up. But the ice refused to budge. By late September, with a bitter gale blowing in the northwest, Parry gave up.

He was bitterly disappointed. He had waited until the last moment, clinging to the belief that a miracle might occur. But there was no miracle. When he called his officers together they all agreed to remain at Igloolik for another winter and try again the following summer. They could not know that it would be eleven months to the day before they could once more break free of the encircling bonds of ice.

CHAPTER FOUR

The People of Igloolik

FOR THE NEXT TEN MONTHS PARRY AND HIS MEN WERE IN ALMOST DAILY CON-
TACT WITH THE TWO HUNDRED INUIT WHO LIVED AT IGLOOLIK. INDEED, THE
MOST VALUABLE THING ABOUT THIS STRANGELY DISAPPOINTING EXPEDITION IS
THE ACCOUNTS THAT PARRY AND LYON BOTH BROUGHT BACK OF THE NATIVES'
CUSTOMS AND SOCIETY. THESE PROVIDED THE BASIS FOR LATER STUDIES OF THE
MELVILLE PENINSULA INUIT.

Both officers were privileged to observe an Aboriginal society
untouched by European civilization. It was a society that had managed to
exist and even thrive in one of the harshest environments on the globe. Of
course, Parry and Lyon weren't anthropologists. Indeed, anthropology—the
scientific study of the human race—didn't exist and wouldn't until the mid-
century. But both were keen observers. They liked the Inuit. In their long
and monotonous confinement they had the time to examine a culture they
found foreign and fascinating.

Of course, they judged the Inuit in terms of their own "civilized" standards. It didn't occur to them—nor would it occur to any Englishman in
that age—that different conditions require different codes of conduct.

Parry discovered that the cheerful Natives "maintained a degree of har-
mony among themselves which is scarcely ever disturbed." That being the
case, he thought, they could only benefit from Christian evangelism. But he
was soon to notice that the Inuit far to the south, who had been "civilized"
and Christianized, had turned into thieves, pilferers, and pickpockets, so
greedy that one even offered to sell his two children for some trade goods.

By contrast, the uncivilized Natives of Southampton Island and the
Melville Peninsula were honest to a fault. If you dropped a handkerchief or
a glove, they ran after you to return it. Sledges could be left unguarded with-

out fear of loss. Lyon once purposely left a stock of knives, scissors, looking glasses, and other coveted objects in a Native hut, and then wandered off, leaving a dozen Natives behind. When he returned, he found his possessions intact and carefully covered with a skin.

To both officers the most unusual aspect of the Inuit character was its lack of passion. They weren't warlike or quarrelsome; these typically European emotions were curiously lacking. Feelings of love and jealousy were also apparently unknown. Lyon felt, in fact, that the Inuit didn't possess much of the milk of human kindness. Sympathy, compassion, gratitude—these qualities didn't appear on the surface.

The Natives cheerfully helped the British ... Their own doors were always open. Their food was always shared with strangers—and they didn't expect any payment.

But there was a reason for this. Death was so much a part of the Inuit life, they had become used to it. In a pitiless land, there was no room for pity. Three days of mourning were allowed after a death and the mourners all cried real tears—but only for a minute. They seemed indifferent to the presence of death. Nobody bothered to cover corpses. The British thought the Inuit callous, but in the Arctic, where exposure, starvation, and disease killed so many so young, no other attitude was possible if sanity was to be maintained.

Parry remarked on what he called the "selfishness of the savage." He thought it one of their greatest failings. The British showered presents on the Natives and fed them when they were near starvation, but were annoyed because nobody said thank you.

Obviously it never occurred to any Inuit to acknowledge a gift or a service because in their own world they had to depend on one another. You helped a man out one day, he helped you out the next. That is the way the Arctic world worked. No one was expected to acknowledge kindness.

The Natives cheerfully helped the British. They hauled water on sledges, they showed them how to build a snow wall around the *Fury*. They drew maps of the coastline. They brought in fresh fish. They expected presents in return, but to say thank you would have been redundant.

Their own doors were always open. Their food was always shared with strangers—and they didn't expect any payment. They accepted tragedy as they accepted death, with indifference, and sometimes even a little laughter and high spirits. A man could leave his dying wife, not caring who looked after her in his absence. A girl could laugh at the suffering of a dying brother. A sick woman could be blockaded inside a snow hut without anybody bothering to discover when she died. Old people with no dependents were simply left to eke out a living or die. This "brutal insensitivity," as Lyon called it, was appalling to the English, who couldn't comprehend the savage conditions faced by the people of Igloolik.

As they discarded pity, they also discarded the harsher emotions. Revenge was unknown to them, as was war. They didn't quarrel among themselves. They couldn't afford the luxury of high passion. They needed to conserve their feelings to wage the daily battle with the wild. They learned to laugh at trouble, and they laughed and grinned a great deal even when life was hard for them, as it usually was. They lived for the day—for any day might be their last.

Parry thought them wasteful and so they were—in his terms. Life for them was feast or famine. When food was available, they ate it all. When there was none, they went without and didn't complain. The British thought them gluttons. But gluttony in that spare land was one of the few luxuries they knew.

They were always thirsty, and when they could they drank vast quantities of water, or other fluids. For raging thirst was as common in the Arctic as in the desert. To eat snow was taboo for whites and Natives alike—the resulting loss of body heat could kill a man. But snow could only rarely be melted because fuel was as precious as food. Water was a luxury to be obtained at great expense.

Parry once conducted an experiment to find out how much a Native could eat. He offered a young Inuit, Tooloak, as much food and drink as he could consume overnight. In just twenty-one hours, eight of which were taken up by sleep, Tooloak tucked away ten and a quarter pounds (4.6 kg) of bread and meat and drank almost two gallons (9 L) of liquid.

The irrepressible Lyon decided to pit his man, Kangara, against Tooloak. Kangara managed to devour in nineteen hours just under ten pounds (4.5 kg) of meat, bread, and candies, and six quarts (6.8 L) of soup and water.

Lyon insisted that if Kangara had been given Tooloak's extra two hours, he would have "beaten him hollow."

To Parry the Native diet was "horrible and disgusting." After all, they ate raw blubber. Lyon, who had nibbled sheep's eyes with a Bedouin of the western desert, wasn't so choosy. Like the Inuit, he ate the half-digested contents of the stomachs of caribou, which they called *nerooka*. He found it "acid and rather pungent, resembling as near as I could judge, a mixture of sorrel and radish leaves." But he didn't think to ask why, nor did he seem to connect this half-digested vegetable diet with the Natives' remarkable freedom from scurvy.

The Natives were just as repelled by British food. They hated sugar. They spat out rum. When one was offered a cup of coffee and a plate of gingerbread, he made a wry face and acted as if he was taking medicine. One miserable woman, who had been left to starve after her husband's death, was brought aboard and offered bread, jelly, and a biscuit. Lyon noticed she threw the food away, only pretending to eat it.

If the Inuit mystified the British with their customs and attitudes, they in turn were confused and baffled by the strange men aboard the big ships. One thing they couldn't understand was why the strangers hadn't brought their wives with them. When told that some had no wives, they were astonished. Surely, they thought, every man in the world had at least one wife!

They couldn't understand a community whose members were not related. In their own society, *everybody* was related by blood, or adoption. To solve that problem, Lyon told them he was father to the whole crew. That, of course, didn't satisfy some of the women who knew that some of his "sons" seemed older than he.

Nor could they understand the British class system. It was clear that Parry and Lyon were important men. The Inuit believed they owned their ships. But the different ranks confused them. In their society everyone was equal. But, in spite of this clash of cultures, the two peoples got along famously. The Inuit were immensely helpful to Parry and his men, who in turn were generous to them.

If the Britons thought of themselves as the Natives' superiors, there is evidence the Inuit thought the opposite. Parry noted that "they certainly looked on us in many respects with profound contempt; maintaining the idea of self sufficiency which has induced them … to call themselves, by way of distinction *Innuee*, or mankind."

To the British, the Inuit were like children—untutored savages who could only benefit from the white man's ways. This attitude was quite unjustified. In the decades that followed, the real children in the Arctic would be the white explorers. Without the Inuit to care for them, hunt for them, and guide them through that chill, inhospitable land, scores more would have died of starvation, scurvy, exhaustion, or exposure.

Without the Inuit, the journeys to seek out the Pole and the Passage would not have been possible. Yet their contribution has been noted only casually. It was the British Navy's loss that it learned so little from the Natives. Had it paid attention, the tragedies that followed might have been averted.

Actually, in most instances the white men were far worse off and much more wretched than the Natives. The Inuit were more practically clothed and more efficiently housed.

Here was a nation obsessed by science, whose explorers were charged with collecting everything from skins of the Arctic tern to the shells that lay on the beaches. Here were men of intelligence with a mania for figures, charts, and statistics, recording everything from the water temperatures to the magnetic forces that surround the Pole. Yet few thought it necessary to inquire into the reasons why another set of fellow humans could survive, year after year, winter after winter, in an environment that strained and often broke the white man's spirit.

The British felt for the Natives. They lamented their wretched condition. And they couldn't understand why, on being offered a trip to civilization, they flatly refused the proposal. Actually, in most instances the white men were far worse off and much more wretched than the Natives. The Inuit were more practically clothed and more efficiently housed. They enjoyed better health than the white explorers, to whom the tough overland expeditions had brought exhaustion and even death.

The Inuit wore loose parkas of fur or sealskin. But the British Navy stuck to the more confining wool, flannel, and broadcloth uniforms with no protective hoods. The Inuit kept their feet warm in sealskin and mukluks.

Even Parry rejected Navy leather. The Inuit sleds were light and flexible. The Navy's were heavy and awkward and hauled by men, not dogs. No naval man ever would learn the technique of dog driving or the art of building a snow house on the trail.

Most puzzling of all was the inability of the Europeans to understand the great Arctic scourge—scurvy—that struck almost every white expedition to the North. The seeds of scurvy were already in Parry's men, in spite of lemon juice and marmalade. Yet no one connected the Inuits' diet with the state of their health. Though the effects of vitamins were unknown, the explorers sensed that scurvy was linked to diet, and that fresh meat and vegetables helped ward it off. But nobody caught on to the truth that raw meat and blubber are very effective antidotes against scurvy.

Why this apparent blindness? Part of it was because the upper classes of England considered themselves superior to most people—whether they were Americans, Africans, or Inuit. Part of it was also fear—the fear of going native. The idea of traipsing about in ragged seal furs, eating raw blubber, and living in hovels built of snow did not appeal to the average Englishman. Those who had done such things in some of the world's distant corners had been despised as misfits who had thrown away the standards of civilization to become wild animals.

Besides, it was considered rather like cheating to do things the easy way. The real triumph consisted of pressing forward against all odds, without ever stooping to adopt the Native style. The British officers enjoyed these people whom they had spent so much time with; but they refused to copy them. And for that they paid a price.

Still, when the Inuit began to leave in the spring in April 1823, Parry and his officers missed their company and perhaps even envied their nomadic life. The Natives were on the move. The white men were imprisoned on their ships, caught fast in the ice.

Parry now decided to send one ship home and carry on alone. But the winter had been appallingly cold. The ice showed no signs of budging. The telltale signs of scurvy—blackened gums, loose teeth, sore joints—were making their appearance. Parry thought that cleanliness and exercise would help stop the disease. In that, he was quite wrong.

August arrived. They were still frozen in. Again, the crews toiled to saw a channel through the ice pack, trying to reach open water. Weakened by illness and by eleven months of being cooped up on the ship, they couldn't work with the same energy. Parry climbed the masthead of his ship and gazed off to the west. And then his heart sank, for as far as he could see the ice stretched off unbroken. Now he knew that he would have to go home without having achieved his goal.

On August 12, he bade goodbye to Igloolik. He had now been hovering off the mouth of that narrow strait for thirteen long months. He was certain that this was the entrance to the Passage. He was sure the open sea lay less than a hundred miles (160 km) to the west. But he couldn't reach it. The ice master of the *Hecla* was already dying of scurvy. Others would follow unless he could get back to civilization.

It wasn't easy. Even when he got out of the ice-locked harbour, and fought his way through the pack, there were holdups. During one period of twenty-six days, there were only two in which he could move ahead. The scurvy patient died before he could get home.

Finally, on October 10, he anchored off Lerwick in the Shetland Islands, to the ringing of bells and the cheers of the inhabitants, who rushed to the wharfside to greet the ships. These were the first white men he and his crew had seen in twenty-seven months. That night the citizens of the little town celebrated by lighting huge barrels of tar on every street.

Alas, Parry's discoveries had been negative. He had learned that there was no route to the Passage by way of Hudson Bay because no ship could squeeze through the ice that clogged the little strait which he named for his two ships—*Fury* and *Hecla*.

Perhaps there were other ways. On the earlier expedition he had ventured briefly down the long fjord he had named for the Prince Regent. Could that be the way? Perhaps at the bottom of the long inlet there was a connection with the mysterious Passage. He would have to mount another expedition to explore that.

His optimism rose. He said he had never felt more sure of ultimate success. He was confident that the English would yet be destined "to succeed in an attempt which has for centuries engaged her attention, and interested the whole civilized world."

In short, he hadn't given up. He was scarcely back home before he was pressing for a third chance to make another voyage. He was obsessed by the mystery of the Passage. Indeed, it obsessed the entire country. No hardship was too unbearable, no years of isolation too stifling, no experience too horrifying to prevent the naval explorers from trying again. One would have thought that a man like Parry might have shrunk from another voyage of dreadful hardships. On the contrary, he was eager to be off.

CHAPTER FIVE

The End of the *Fury*

IN SPITE OF HIS OPTIMISM, IN THE MONTHS THAT FOLLOWED PARRY WAS AT A LOW POINT. ON HIS RETURN TO ENGLAND, HE LEARNED THAT HIS FATHER HAD DIED. HE WAS SO DEPRESSED HE COULDN'T EAT OR EVEN SPEAK. HIS SISTER RUSHED TO HIS LONDON HOTEL TO FIND HIM DELIRIOUS WITH HIGH FEVER. HIS CONDITION WAS KEPT FROM HIS MOTHER UNTIL THE CRISIS PASSED.

If that weren't enough, he learned that Miss Browne, with whom he had flirted aboard his ship, and with whom he was said to have an understanding, had lost interest in him. One could hardly blame her. She hadn't seen him since that spring, two and a half years before. But now her mother was going about claiming he had abandoned her.

Parry was miserable. But then he learned that Miss Browne had been seen in the company of other men in his absence. In fact she had actually got engaged to somebody else. And though her mother was trying to get the two together again, Parry wasn't having any of that. In fact, the knowledge of Miss Browne's shocking conduct (shocking to the people of those days only) cured his melancholy.

At the same time he was being praised by the best and brightest in England—all the way from Britain's leading scientist, Sir Humphrey Davy, to Sir Thomas Lawrence, the society painter, and Robert Peel, future prime minister.

He continued to be worried about his future. He really had not been very successful in his quest for the Passage—even though he had gone farther than any other white man. The Navy offered him a minor job, but not as an explorer. But then, in the first week of January 1824, the decision was made that he sail north again on his quest. Once again, the *Hecla* and the *Fury* would be under his command.

He was determined to be married. And he quickly fell in love with the nearest available candidate, a young woman named Jemima Symes, who was conveniently living at his mother's house in Bath. She was very ill and her condition wasn't helped by the fact that Parry was more anxious to be off to the frozen ocean than he was to be with her. But, for the moment at least, she fitted the role of future partner for which the explorer clearly longed.

At Deptford, the *Hecla* again drew crowds; she was now the most famous ship in the Navy. In the three months before Parry sailed, some three thousand persons signed the visitors' register. They came from all over the British islands, and as far away as Vienna. The well-wishers included Prince Leopold of Saxe-Cobourg, the uncle of the future prince consort, two royal duchesses, and, on the last day, the family of Sir John Stanley of Alderley, whose daughter, Isabella, would one day be Parry's wife.

He was determined to be married. And he quickly fell in love with the nearest available candidate, a young woman named Jemima Symes, who was conveniently living at his mother's house in Bath.

That April, another future Arctic wife, Jane Griffin, (who would marry Sir John Franklin) met Parry at a dinner party and described him to her journal, as "a fine looking man of commanding appearance, but possessing nothing of the fine gentleman … his figure is rather slouching, his face full & round, his hair dark & rather curling." To her, he seemed "far from light hearted & exhibits traces of heartfelt & recent suffering, in spite of which he occasionally bursts into hearty laughter & seems to enjoy a joke."

She thought Parry was going back north against his own wishes, complaining to her he had seen nothing of the rest of the world. But this peculiar English reluctance was a mask. He was raring to go, but he didn't want to show it publicly. An Englishman in those days mustn't appear too keen; it just wasn't done.

His orders were clear. He was to sail down Prince Regent Inlet, which he had only partially explored on his first voyage. There he was to look for a channel west which would connect with the coastline which John Franklin, his naval colleague, had explored in 1821. If that could be done, he felt, the Passage was as good as conquered.

Again he reckoned without the changeable Arctic weather. He was faced with another 150 miles (241 km) of jostling icebergs in Baffin Bay, all jammed together, imprisoning both his vessels and threatening to crush them like eggshells. He had expected to work his way through in a month, as he had in 1819. It took him more than two.

At last, on September 10, he reached Lancaster Sound again, a month behind schedule. Three days later, only twenty miles (32 km) from the entrance to Prince Regent Inlet, the ships were again caught in the ice. The season was almost over. Now he faced a difficult choice: should he try to make a retreat to England? To Parry that was unthinkable—an admission of defeat.

He determined to push on west as far as possible and try to get to the Passage the following year. But a gale drove him back down the sound and right into Baffin Bay. Then the wind changed and the second gale blew the two ships back again.

He was able to find a wintering place at last on the northwest shore of Baffin Island, in the small bay off Prince Regent Inlet. And for the next ten months this bleak coastline would be his home.

He had never encountered a gloomier landscape. There were no cheerful Natives here to while away the dreary hours. No animal was seen. Even the gulls that fluttered around the ship were gone. The white plain was as empty of life as it was of colour.

But of course he had prepared for that. There would be costume parties and grand balls, in which men and officers frolicked together in fancy dress. Discipline was relaxed to a certain extent. For the Grand Venetian Carnival, Parry climbed down the *Hecla*'s side enveloped in a large cloak that he did not throw off until all were assembled on the *Fury*'s deck. To the delight of the company, he stood revealed as an old mariner with a wooden leg, whom his sailors recognized as the man who played the fiddle on the road near Chatham back home.

Parry, the amateur actor, kept up the role, scraping on a fiddle, and crying out, "Give a copper to poor Joe, your Honour, who's lost his timbers in defence of his King and country!"

Not to be outdone, his second-in-command, Lieutenant Henry Hoppner, appeared as a lady of fashion, with a black footman in livery, who was revealed to be Francis Crozier, a midshipman aboard the *Hecla*.

And so they capered to the music of their captain's fiddle—monks in cowls, Turkish dancers, chimney sweeps, ribbon girls, and rag men, Highland warriors, dandies, bricklayers and farmers, tropical princesses, and match girls, whirling about in quadrilles, waltzes, and country dances—a bright pinpoint of revelry in the sullen Arctic night.

On July 20, 1825, they were freed at last from their winter harbour and set sail for the western shore of the great inlet. Now Parry had felt the real voyage had commenced. They were passing shores that had never been explored. The prospect of a speedy passage seemed bright.

But once more the Arctic blocked them. Hugging the shore of Somerset Island, whose crumbling cliffs sent masses of limestone tumbling onto a mountain of rubble at their base, they ran into a stiff gale. On July 30, it grounded the *Fury* on an exposed and narrow beach. She was scarcely hauled free when both ships were trapped.

*A huge iceberg forced the **Fury** against a mass of grounded ice, threatening to tear her to pieces. She trembled violently. Beams and timbers cracked. A crash like a gunshot was heard and her rudder was half torn away.*

A huge iceberg forced the *Fury* against a mass of grounded ice, threatening to tear her to pieces. She trembled violently. Beams and timbers cracked. A crash like a gunshot was heard and her rudder was half torn away. She began to leak badly, but there was no landing place safe enough to make repairs. All her crew could do was to pray to keep her from drowning again and to work the four pumps in shifts until their hands were raw and bleeding.

For two weeks officers and crew sought to save the ship. They tried to tie her to an iceberg, but the bergs were wasted by weather and the cables snapped. They tried to raise her to examine her battered keel, but a blizzard stopped them. Both ships were in danger of being smashed against the headland. Nothing seemed to work.

The crews had reached the breaking point, so exhausted that some fell into a stupor, unable to understand an order. On August 21, Parry was forced to cast off his own ship, *Hecla,* to save her from being driven aground. The same gale drove the *Fury* onto the beach and blocked her exit with huge bergs. It became obvious she would have to be abandoned.

That caused Parry great pain. Everything about this expedition had been a failure. He hadn't found the Passage—hadn't gotten near it. He had explored no more than a few miles of new land. Now he had lost his ship— the one catastrophe the Navy would find hard to forgive.

He sailed off with the *Hecla* crammed with a double complement of officers and men. He left her sister ship and most of its stores on the beach—Fury Beach it would be called. Perhaps, he thought, these provisions might help some future expedition.

On October 16, 1825, Parry was home with nothing to show for sixteen months of cold and exertion. At the court martial that followed, all were acquitted and the officers praised and flattered. Parry was relieved, but the fact remained: he'd lost his ship.

Now he decided never again to seek the elusive North West Passage. He wanted to be free of complications.

Jemima Symes was happy to see him safe. She was still sick, but cheerful. However, the relationship came to an end. But Parry still hungered for a wife. "I have always felt a desire to be attached to somewhere," he wrote a friend. "I have never been easy without it, and with less disposition I will venture to say, than 99 in 100 of my own profession, to vicious propensities, either in this or other ways. I have always contrived to fancy myself in love with some virtuous woman. There is some romance in this, but I have it still in full force within me, and never, till I am married, shall I, I believe, cease to entertain it."

His general loneliness, his hunger for love and marriage, and the knowledge of his failure brought on depression. He suffered from headaches. He took drugs to help him. Now he decided never again to seek the elusive North West Passage. He wanted to be free of complications.

He wrote another polar book—a single volume this time and not nearly as long. It did not meet with the chorus of cheers that had greeted his earlier works. Critics were unenthusiastic, for it was clear that nothing had been accomplished on this last expedition.

Parry had said he would never go north again, that he was through with the Arctic. But those were hasty sentiments, uttered at the end of a long and dispiriting battle with the ice. It began to dawn on him that there was one way to restore his battered reputation, by another daring attempt. If not to seek the fabled Passage, then why not the North Pole itself?

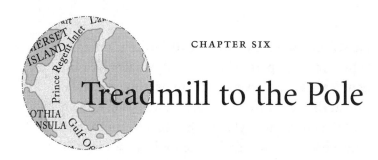

CHAPTER SIX

Treadmill to the Pole

BY THE SPRING OF 1826 WILLIAM EDWARD PARRY HAD FALLEN IN LOVE AGAIN.
HE HAD REVERSED HIS DECISION TO ABANDON ARCTIC EXPLORATION. THE
OPTIMISTIC EXPLORER WAS SURE HE COULD REACH THE NORTH POLE IN A SIN-
GLE SEASON. MEANWHILE HE HAD ASKED SIR JOHN STANLEY OF ALDERLEY FOR
HIS DAUGHTER'S HAND IN MARRIAGE.

He had met Isabella Stanley through his friend Edward, Isabella's brother. He was clearly seeking a wife when Isabella, a zesty twenty-four-year-old,
fragile looking in the style of the period, but undeniably beautiful, was
available. By May he was in love, and sure enough of her agreement to
approach her father.

Of course, he didn't use the word "love" to Sir John. It would, perhaps,
have been considered crude in those formal days, to admit to something so
unrefined as passion. He simply said he was "irresistibly drawn towards …
Isabella by sentiments much warmer than those of common esteem and
regard …"

After two agonizing months the Stanleys gave in. The two were married
in October. At the same time Lord Melbourne, the first lord of Admiralty,
agreed that Parry could pursue his quest for the North Pole.

For Isabella any separation would be agony, and she knew that a long
and agonizing parting was to come. Parry expected to leave England in the
Hecla in April of 1827 for weeks, months, perhaps even years. He remained
the incurable optimist. He was convinced he could reach the Pole by way of
Norway in a single season and ignored the experts, who told him how difficult it would be.

The old whaling captain, William Scoresby, now entered the picture.
Scoresby wasn't nearly as enthusiastic as Parry was about anybody's ability

to reach the Pole in a single season. Scoresby was an extraordinary man—perhaps the most remarkable Arctic expert of his day. A whaler like his father, he had been eighteen years at sea, seven of them as a master. He'd been given his first command at the age of twenty-one and was soon known as the bravest and smartest of the Greenland whalers. But he was more than that. In the winters, when the whaling season ended, he took classes in philosophy and science at Edinburgh. And he was inventive. One of his inventions was a pair of "ice shoes" for walking more easily across the rough ice pack.

> *Scoresby was an extraordinary man — perhaps the most remarkable Arctic expert of his day. A whaler like his father, he had been eighteen years at sea, seven of them as a master.*

He produced a paper on polar ice conditions, and also a monumental work which has been called "one of the most remarkable books in the English language" as well as the "foundation stone of Arctic science."

Now this old-time whaler with the weathered face had become an ordained minister. He scorned those who believed there was an Open Polar Sea north of the ice pack. The idea that beyond that wall of ice was a warm ocean was one no Greenland whaler could accept. They could all see the wall of ice. Why should it suddenly vanish in a colder climate?

But Scoresby was snubbed by the Royal Navy, which had no use for whalers. This was a snobbish attitude. The men who ran the Navy felt that they were the best people for the job. But Scoresby had far more experience. He had once tried to take part in that first expedition to the Arctic with Parry and Ross. But the Navy had refused to allow that. Now, when he tried to issue some warnings about Arctic travel, Parry and the Navy ignored him.

Scoresby had already made it clear the best mode of travel in the Arctic was by light flexible sledges built on slender wooden frames and covered with waterproof skins—the kind the Natives used. These should be pulled by either reindeer or dogs, preferably dogs.

He also warned that any expedition seeking the Pole must set out on the ice when it was frozen hard and was relatively flat, in late April or early May. Later on when the weather warmed, huge pools formed and hummocks appeared and slush covered the surface, making travel difficult.

Scoresby had sixty thousand miles (96,500 km) of experience travelling through the ice behind him. He had also gone farther north than any other white explorer. But Parry ignored him. He built two heavy boat-sleds, each seventy feet (21.3 m) long, with a twenty-foot (6-m) beam, weighing three-quarters of a ton (680 kg) and equipped with steel runners so that they could be dragged over the ice. He didn't take dogs, and the reindeer he bought were never used.

Nor did he take the whaler's advice about making an early start. He didn't plan to set off across the ice until the first of June. Even that late deadline was missed. Imprisoned in the floes of Spitzbergen well to the north of Norway, he spent ten precious days seeking a safe harbour for the *Hecla* and didn't get away until June 21. Yet he continued to be optimistic. "The main object of our exercise appeared almost within our grasp," he wrote.

He was deeply in love with his new wife. It had been a wrench to part with Isabella and even more wrenching for her, since she found herself pregnant. She couldn't write to him so she kept a diary in which she wrote

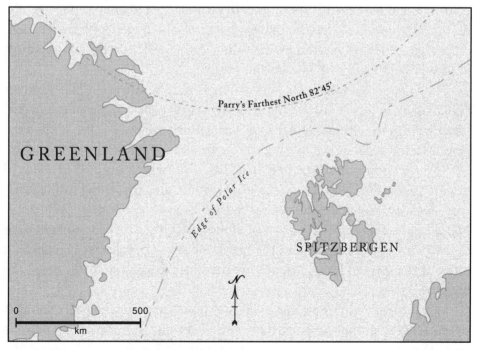

Parry's last voyage: toward the Pole, 1827

down her own feelings. She yearned for his presence that spring and spoke to him through her diary: "I would not recall you, your path leads to glory and honour and never would I turn you from that path when I feel and know it as a path you ought to go …"

But the path that Parry had chosen was rough. He expected to find the smooth, flat expanse of ice that some whalers reported. It didn't occur to him, as Scoresby had indicated, that that condition only existed in the early months of the year before the weather changed and the ice grew rougher. Why hadn't he taken the old whaler's advice? Probably because the Navy, snobbish in the extreme, had no use for whalers.

The Navy actually believed that beyond the icy barriers there lay an Open Polar Sea—a ring of warm water surrounding the Pole. That was one reason, no doubt, why Parry built heavy boats rather than the light sledges Scoresby had suggested. The theory of an Open Polar Sea was nonsense. Scoresby didn't believe it for a minute, and when he heard it discussed he flatly predicted that Parry would never reach the Pole.

Parry and his second-in-command, James Clark Ross, a nephew of the discredited John Ross, set off, each in charge of a boat-sled with twelve men. Once again, they were unlucky with the weather. The season was the most unfavourable they could have encountered.

They had never seen such rain. Twenty times as much fell that summer as had fallen in any of the seven previous summers he'd spent in the Arctic. It came down in torrents—once for a steady thirty hours. But then, when the sun came out it shone so hot that the tar ran out of the seams of the boats.

The rain and warm weather turned the ice into a rumpled expanse of broken cakes, all piled one on top of the other, and stretching to the horizon—high, sharp masses that impeded every step of the men. It was like trying to haul a cart through a yard of stones, with the stones ten times their normal dimensions. It was also the "penknife ice"—needle-like crystals that tore out the soles of boots. And there was slush, knee deep, that caused the men to go down on all fours.

When there wasn't rain there was fog. It was so thick the party couldn't see and had to grope along, yard by yard, from one hummock of ice to the next, trying to avoid the thousands of ponds that formed between the blocks.

The need to launch and land the boats, and to load and unload and reload them, and to make circuits around the ponds slowed the expedition to a snail's pace. Parry had hoped to make thirteen miles (21 km) a day. He could scarcely make half a mile (800 m). On one occasion it took two hours to move a hundred yards (91 m).

He expected to meet what he called "the main ice"—the smooth continuous plain the whalers had described. He couldn't get it into his head that in summer that didn't exist. His men were wet and exhausted. Their rations were scanty. Parry hadn't brought enough food for the men who were performing hard labour for ten hours.

But there was a worse problem. A stiff wind blowing down from the Pole was driving the ice backwards. At last, Parry understood what the whaling captains always knew—that even as his party plodded grimly north, the ice was moving south. In short, they were on a treadmill. For every step they took forward, the ice took them one step back.

His men were suffering from chilblains, snow blindness, and scurvy. By the time they reached the first solid land, they had been fifty-six hours without rest and couldn't understand orders.

On July 26, Parry realized that, though they seemed to have moved ten or eleven miles (16 to 17.7 km) north, they were actually three miles (4.8 km) *south* of their starting point that day. He didn't tell the men. They thought they were pressing close to the eighty-third parallel at which they would receive a thousand-pound reward that Parliament offered to anyone who got that far.

Two days later Parry had to give up. His instruments told him that he had managed to reach the hitherto unattainable latitude of 82°45'—a quarter degree farther than anybody else had ever made it. It was a considerable achievement and it would stand for fifty years, adding to Parry's towering reputation as the greatest of the Arctic explorers.

But if he had taken the despised Scoresby's advice he would have achieved more. He and his party had clocked 978 miles (1,574 km) of polar travel, but because of the circuitous route, the need to shovel supplies back and forth, and the southward movement of the ice, he was only 178 miles (286 km) north of the harbour where he had anchored his ship.

And he couldn't go on. His men were suffering from chilblains, snow blindness, and scurvy. By the time they reached the first solid land, they had been fifty-six hours without rest and couldn't understand orders. Parry noted that they had "a wildness in their looks." They recovered and reached the ship on August 21 after an absence of sixty-one days.

Once again Parry had missed his target. It would have been easier if the Admiralty hadn't felt it necessary to announce he was going to the Pole. "I wish I could say we have been successful but this we have not," he wrote to his wife. He was crazy with desire to "clasp my dear girl to my heart."

As he approached London, he grew more impatient. He landed at Inverness and was held up at Durham for lack of horses. The Duke of Wellington, travelling the same road, had commandeered all available transport. Parry used the delay to express "the unspeakable joy and comfort" his wife's letter had given him. He had received it at Edinburgh the previous night. All the problems of the polar trip vanished when he learned for the first time that he was to become a father.

In a very real way, the birth of his child compensated him for his lack of success. As he wrote Isabella, "success in my enterprise is by no means essential to our joy, tho' it might have added something to it; but we cannot, ought not to have *everything* we wish …"

However, in spite of his failure—or perhaps because he had gone farther north than any other white man—he was knighted and became Sir Edward Parry. He stubbornly insisted that although the Pole would be more difficult to reach than anybody had previously believed, he could not himself "recommend any material improvement in the plan lately adopted." But that flew in the face of all reason and experience.

It was certainly too much for William Scoresby, the whaler, who publicly recorded his disagreement, pointing out that Inuit invariably used dogs and light sledges and that their light boats were only thirty feet (9 m) long and carried as many passengers as Parry's. Moreover, they could be hoisted on the backs of six or eight men.

The Native boat weighed between four and five hundred pounds (181 to 226 kg); Parry's weighed 1,450 (658 kg). It would be many years before the British Navy finally began to adopt Inuit methods of travel in the north, using light sledges and dogs.

This was Parry's last expedition. He settled down now as the first of the explorer heroes and a member of the famous Arctic Council of senior explorers, which had so much to do with the future exploration of the frozen world. Parry was hailed as the greatest explorer of his day. He had actually gone farther into the Arctic than any other man and farther towards the North Pole than any other white man. Both these records stood for decades.

On that first remarkable expedition luck was with him. In the last his luck failed. But his good fortune and his bad fortune were both tied to vagaries of Arctic weather. He got as far as he did on that first expedition because the weather was on his side. He failed on his second, because the weather was against him.

He was, above all, an optimist. He thought he could go where no man had gone before, and he succeeded. But he also thought he could go farther and in that he failed. When he set out for the Arctic he knew nothing of the Arctic channels or the Arctic conditions. He learned, but he might have learned more had he listened to the Natives and observed their techniques.

In that he was very much a product of his time. He was an Englishman and an amateur with all the amateur Englishman's self-confidence and arrogance. It was both his strength and his weakness.

It's ironic that both of the goals that he was seeking on his failed quests turned out to have very little practical meaning. The North West Passage certainly existed. John Franklin came upon it, but died before he could report it. Robert McClure discovered it and got through it, partly by boat and partly on foot. It wasn't until 1905 that Roald Amundsen went all the way from Lancaster Sound to the Bering Sea—eighty-seven years after Parry's trip to Melville Island.

But the North West Passage had no practical use. Even today with modern icebreakers it's difficult and sometimes impossible to force a ship through that tangle of ice-choked channels. From a commercial point of view it has no value.

And the North Pole? It's simply a pinpoint on the map—a bit of frozen ocean that has, again, no practical value. The nineteenth-century British explorers sought it the same way later explorers once sought to climb Mount Everest—because it was there.

Parry's real contribution, surely, is his careful observations of Inuit life in the days before white civilization changed that way of life forever. His reports and those of his subordinate, Lyon, give us an insight into a remarkable people who, unlike so many white explorers, managed to survive in a dreadful environment. Parry's reputation lies as much in his observations of these cheerful Aboriginals as it does in his attempts to seek the will-o'-the-wisp of the mysterious Passage. He learned *about* the Inuit; what a shame he didn't learn *from* them.

INDEX

An illustration of relics found with the bodies of
Franklin's crew, from the *Illustrated London News,*
October 15, 1859.

(COURTESY LIBRARY AND ARCHIVES CANADA, NLC-000734)

JANE FRANKLIN'S OBSESSION

CONTENTS

The Mysterious Passage

EVER SINCE NORTH AMERICA WAS DISCOVERED, SEAMEN OF ALL NATIONS HOPED TO FIND A WATER HIGHWAY, CUTTING THROUGH THE CENTRE OF THE CONTINENT OF NORTH AMERICA. THEY WERE SURE IT WOULD LEAD ON TO ASIA— THAT MYSTERIOUS REALM OF RICHES: SPICES, SILKS, TREASURE OF ALL KINDS.

A passage through the continent would provide a short cut that would cut weeks, even months, off the regular voyage. At last they would be able to avoid the long round-about routes that led through the dreadful storms at the foot of the South American continent—Cape Horn—or the equally difficult passage at the foot of Africa—The Cape of Good Hope.

But no such easy shortcut to the Orient existed. That became obvious as explorers and fur traders began to work their way across the continent and farther and farther north through Canada. If a passage did exist, it was to be found only beyond the cold mists of the Arctic.

There were some, indeed, who didn't think there could be a passage. They believed that the continent continued on north until it reached the North Pole. Others felt that there might be an ocean at the top of the continent which would be easily navigable. Others were convinced—and more rightly—that a maze of islands and wriggling channels would be found in the Arctic Ocean north of the top of North America. Perhaps these channels might form a passage that could be navigated, and the Orient reached.

From the days of Queen Elizabeth I to the twentieth century, Englishmen sought to find such a passage. One of these was a plump naval officer named John Franklin, the best known of all Arctic explorers. Much of the credit for his fame belongs to his wife, the remarkable Lady Jane Franklin. It was she who kept his memory alive after others tended to forget it.

Franklin was only one of a long line of British seamen who had vainly sought the mysterious Passage. The quest had obsessed and frustrated English sailors and explorers for almost three hundred years. As one of them, Martin Frobisher, declared, "It is *still* the only thing left undone, whereby a notable mind might be made famous and remarkable." Anybody who could find the Passage, in short, would be a hero, and a wealthy one.

Frobisher, a friend of both Drake and Hawkins, famous sea dogs who had helped defeat the Spanish Armada, was the first Englishman to seek the Passage. He made three voyages between 1576 and 1578. He was an optimistic man—a little too optimistic as it turned out. He was sure that the "strait" that he had discovered north of the Ungava Peninsula led westward to the Pacific and that a fortune in gold lay on an island near its mouth. His backers were more interested in gold than in exploring. But the gold turned out to be "fool's gold"—iron pyrites. So Frobisher never managed to explore his strait, which we now know was only a bay on the southeast shore of Baffin Island.

Seven years after Frobisher, a more hard-headed Elizabethan sailor, John Davis, a friend of Sir Walter Raleigh, tried again. He rediscovered the great island of Greenland. Incredibly, this huge land mass had been totally forgotten after the failure of the Norse colonies three centuries before. After realizing that Greenland really *did* exist and wasn't a myth, Davis crossed the ice-choked strait that bears his name. There he charted the east coast of a new land, which we now call Baffin Island. He, too, was convinced the mysterious passage existed. But he couldn't get any farther north because a wall of ice barred his way.

Like Frobisher before him, Davis had noticed a broad stretch of water just north of Ungava at the tip of what is now Quebec. It was through this strait that Henry Hudson sailed in 1610; it now bears his name. Hudson burst out onto an apparently limitless sea, and thought he had reached the Pacific Ocean. He was wrong.

It was there, after a dreadful winter, that he met his death at the hands of a mutinous crew, four of whom were later murdered in a skirmish with the Natives. You may have seen the famous painting of Hudson and his son being set adrift to die in the bay that now bears his name.

Those who survived the skirmish with the Natives were brought home by Hudson's first mate, Robert Bylot. That feat of seamanship was so extraordinary that he was pardoned for the mutiny. He made two more voyages to the great bay, and came to believe, rightly, that no navigable passage leading to the Pacific could be found on its western shores.

In 1616, Bylot, refusing to give up, made a fourth Arctic voyage. His pilot was a brilliant seaman named William Baffin, from whom Baffin Island takes its name. They actually got through the ice that had stopped Davis. They travelled three hundred miles (483 km) farther north than he had—a record that stood for more than two centuries.

The two seamen also mapped the entire bay that now bears Baffin's name. They found three openings in that bay, any one of which might lead to unknown lands. These deep sounds were all navigable. The time would come when they would play their part in the exploration of the frozen world. Two openings actually led to the North West Passage, and the third was the gateway to the North Pole.

After this, interest in the Passage dwindled. When Luke Foxe came home in 1631 after exploring Foxe Channel and Foxe Basin north of Hudson Bay, he insisted there could be no route to the Orient south of the Arctic Circle. That killed all hope of a commercially practical passage.

A century later there was a brief flurry when a man named Christopher Middleton explored the west coast of the great island of Southampton in Hudson Bay. He thought he had found a channel which might lead to the Passage, but it wasn't a channel at all, it was only a bay. He ruefully named it Repulse Bay, because it had repulsed him. Oddly enough, a century later it again became a target for those aiming at the secret of the Passage. But Repulse Bay repulsed them too.

Just as the Elizabethans had forgotten about the existence of Greenland, so the British in the early 1800s had forgotten about the whereabouts of Frobisher's discoveries. Even more astonishing, they had disputed whether there really *was* a Baffin Bay. That, in spite of the fact that whaling ships had been operating in Davis Strait for two centuries, and had undoubtedly gone into the bay. In spite of that, the bay was removed from the maps of the time.

Indeed, except for Hudson Bay and part of Baffin Island, the Arctic region was a blank on the map. Even the northern coastline of North

America remained a mystery. Only two overland explorers had managed to reach the Arctic waters—Samuel Hearne, at the Coppermine's mouth in 1771, and Alexander Mackenzie at the Mackenzie Delta in 1789.

But from the tip of Russian Alaska to the shores of Hudson Bay, *everything*, except for these two pinpoints, was uncharted and mysterious. And one thing was now certain: if somewhere in that fog-shrouded realm, a passage linking the oceans was found to exist, it couldn't be much more than a curiosity.

In spite of this, the British Admiralty, in the early nineteenth century, sent ship after ship into the Arctic, searching for the North West Passage. Why? The answer is that the Navy had to find something for its ships and its men and, most important, for its officers to do. For Europe was now at peace. Britain controlled the seas. The wars with France were over. The Emperor Napoleon had been packed off to exile. There were no wars left for the Royal Navy to fight. The new enemy would be the elements themselves. And so the British Navy set out to explore the world. And John Franklin was one of the explorers.

CHAPTER ONE

A Matter of Honour

JANE FRANKLIN WAS ONE OF THE MOST REMARKABLE ENGLISH WOMEN OF THE NINETEENTH CENTURY—AS REMARKABLE AND AS FAMOUS AS QUEEN VICTORIA OR FLORENCE NIGHTINGALE.

She was known internationally and admired because, having helped to send her husband to his death in the Arctic wastes, she devoted more than ten years of her life to push the search for him. And she had a better sense than the professionals of where he might be found. She was determined to enshrine his name as one of the great Arctic heroes. In that she certainly succeeded.

Of the scores of explorers—British, American, Scandinavian, and German—who plunged into the polar wilderness, searching for the mysterious North West Passage, Franklin is by far the best known. His is the name in the school books. His is the name that springs to mind when the North West Passage is mentioned. Franklin in death succeeded where he had failed in life. The mystery of his disappearance raised him from minor Arctic hero to near sainthood. He became the symbol of nineteenth-century Arctic exploration. Had he failed and survived, he would be half forgotten. Today, every schoolchild knows him—and most of the credit for that belongs to his widow.

Because of Jane's stubborn insistence that the search for Franklin and his missing crew be continued, the Arctic was opened up, its channels and islands were explored, charted, mapped, and named. When he vanished into the mists of Lancaster Sound, the world to the north of the Arctic coastline was all but unknown. When the mystery of his fate was finally unravelled, the Arctic was no longer an unknown quantity.

Jane Franklin was thirty-six years old when she married him on

December 5, 1828. Before she met John Franklin she'd turned down many suitors. Perhaps she felt that this was her last chance, though there is no evidence that she did not love and admire him. Certainly she worked hard to forward his career in the Navy.

She was not typical of her sex in an era when women spent their time at needlework or at society balls. She thirsted after wisdom: in one three-year period, she devoured 295 books. She was incurably restless and travelled a great deal. She kept a thick journal in which she noted everything in her cramped, spidery hand. At the age of nineteen, she had worked out a plan to organize her time and enrich her mind, with every moment given over to some form of study.

She was never still. She seemed to belong to everything. She was a member of the Book Society, took lectures at the Royal Institution, visited the Newgate Prison, attended meetings of the British and Foreign School Society, and had opinions on everything.

When she met John Franklin, he was already famous as an Arctic explorer who had tried to reach the North Pole (unsuccessfully) and charted most of the Arctic coast from Alaska to the Coppermine. But Franklin's two overland expeditions to the Arctic were not without tragedy.

She thirsted after wisdom: in one three-year period, she devoured 295 books. She was incurably restless and travelled a great deal. She kept a thick journal in which she noted everything in her cramped, spidery hand.

The first, in fact, had been a disaster. Much of it had to do with his own reckless ambition, his hunger for fame and promotion. For he had set off blindly across the barren ground of British North America without any experience.

That was in 1819 when he was thirty-three years old. He was plump, unaccustomed to hard work, and inexperienced in land travel. He'd been weak and sickly as a child—not expected to live past the age of three. He had little humour and not much imagination.

But he was certainly dogged and certainly brave—calm when danger threatened, courageous in battle. He'd gone to sea at twelve, joined the Navy at fifteen, had taken part in three of the most important battles in the Napoleonic Wars, and had been wounded badly. He had even been shipwrecked, and later rescued. He'd seen his best friend shot to death as he chatted on the deck of one of Nelson's ships, and he had survived when thirty-three out of forty officers were wounded or killed. One bombardment left him partially deaf.

He had been picked to survey the northern coast of North America because he'd gone on a brief expedition to seek the North Pole a year or so before. That expedition had been a failure. And, in fact, there was little about that trip that could prepare him for the swift rivers of the tundra. He had no canoeing experience, no hunting experience, no backpacking experience. But then, no other naval officer had that either.

The hard muscles required of Canadian voyageurs were looked down upon by those officers who trod the quarterdeck of a ship of the line. The Navy simply assumed its officers could do anything. It sent Franklin off to the wilds with little preparation and a minimum of equipment, and expected him and his companions to cover five thousand miles (8,050 km) by foot and canoe, and pick up what they needed from trading posts along the way. In those days, British officers did not stoop to menial tasks. All the hard work was done by the men under their command—ordinary seamen, voyageurs, and Natives. This inability to share the workload on small expeditions such as Franklin's was more than wasteful—it was dangerous. But old customs die hard, and the Royal Navy was the most rigid of the armed services.

Franklin's first North American expedition led him from Great Slave Lake to the Coppermine River, and thence to the Arctic coast. He explored the coast west as far as he could, and then headed back to Great Slave Lake again. The results, however, were disastrous. His party of twenty, including eleven voyageurs, was far too large for its hunters to feed. In spite of that, and in spite of the fact that he only had fifteen days of supplies left, Franklin, ambitious to chart as much territory as possible and perhaps find the Passage, pushed on until he was down to two bags of pemmican and a meal of dried meat.

His paddlers were close to panic. It was clearly madness to continue. Shipwreck and starvation faced them. But Franklin ignored common sense. It seemed to him that the stretch of sea water that he had discovered at the northern tip of the continent might easily be part of the North West

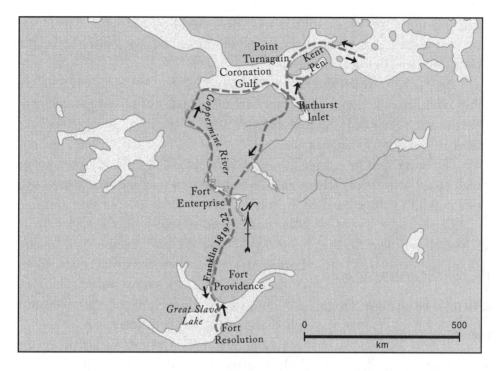

Franklin's First North American Expedition with Back and Richardson, 1819–22

Passage—that it might link up with the Atlantic Ocean to the east, and the Pacific Ocean to the west. But when he reached a point called Point Turnagain, he had to give up.

He knew there wasn't a moment to lose, and yet he wasted five days on the Kent Peninsula seeking an Inuit settlement where he hoped the expedition could spend the winter. That proved impossible, and so he was forced to retreat. It was now late August, with the winter coming on. They tried to make it part of the way by ocean, but mountainous waves forced them to abandon the water route. To get back to their base on Great Slave Lake, they would have to travel overland for 320 miles (515 km).

The trip that followed was a horror. Franklin was the first to faint from lack of food—a few swallows of soup brought him around. But by mid-September the men were used to eating singed hides and a few lichens scraped from the rocks. Five days later he found he couldn't keep up.

They abandoned their canoes—a mistake, as it turned out. The

Coppermine River blocked their way. How could they cross it? They were surviving on old shoes and scraps of untanned leather, enriched by the occasional meal of deer meat.

They tried to reach the river on a raft of willows. It took a week before they could cross in a makeshift canoe that they made of bits of painted canvas in which their bedding was wrapped. One of the Inuit interpreters vanished and was never seen again.

The party split into three groups. One went off to try and find Indians who could help them. The remainder split in two on October 6, when two of Franklin's voyageurs died. Another was too weak to continue and two others offered to stay with him.

Franklin himself was near death when the Indians arrived to save his life. In total he had lost eleven men from starvation and almost died in the process himself.

Franklin and the rest stumbled on toward Fort Enterprise, their original post. Four couldn't make it and tried to move back to the previous camp. There, one of the voyageurs killed one of Franklin's officers.

Franklin himself was near death when the Indians arrived to save his life. In total he had lost eleven men from starvation and almost died in the process himself. But when he returned to England, he was a hero, known as the man who had eaten his boots. In fact his men would not have died had Franklin been more cautious and less ambitious.

One would have thought that this would be enough for Franklin, but it wasn't. He was eager to set off again in spite of his harrowing experience. But before he went he married his first wife, Eleanor Porden, a lively young poet, who, unfortunately, was suffering from tuberculosis. They were married in 1823 but they had less than twenty-three months of married life together.

Franklin was so eager to be back on another expedition to explore the Arctic coastline that he decided to leave, even though his wife was growing weaker day by day. In fact, she had drawn up her will and set her personal affairs in order. Just six days after he left, she died. He didn't get the news until he was deep in the heart of British North America.

In spite of this tragedy, he and his colleagues managed to explore a great section of the Arctic coast of North America—everything that lay between

Russian Alaska and Coronation Gulf near the Coppermine. In fact, he had opened up most of the Arctic coastline of North America, leaving a gap of only 150 miles (240 km) to be explored. Was this the route of the Passage? Franklin could not know, nor could anybody else. Twenty years would pass before he entered the Arctic again.

When he returned home, he was forty-two years old and a widower. He quickly married his wife's friend, Jane Griffin. She would soon be Lady Franklin, for a grateful government would knight her husband for his explorations.

CHAPTER TWO

The Man Who Wouldn't Hurt a Fly

ONE WONDERS WHAT JANE FRANKLIN, WHO WAS QUITE THE OPPOSITE OF HER NEW HUSBAND, SAW IN HIM. PERHAPS IT WAS HIS GENIALITY. HE WAS A GOOD-HEARTED MAN, WHO LITERALLY WOULDN'T HURT A FLY. "THE WORLD IS WIDE ENOUGH FOR BOTH," HE'D SAY, AS HE BLEW THE INSECT OFF HIS HAND WHILE TAKING OBSERVATIONS.

He had many friends and no enemies. Everybody liked him—liked his humility, liked his affectionate and easy nature. He was extremely religious. He read his Bible daily, prayed morning and night, and wouldn't even write a letter on Sunday.

His obvious willingness to be handled by a stronger personality must have been part of his attraction for Jane. But if her will was the stronger of the two, she was clever enough never to show it.

His mood, she noted, was easier than her own. For she saw herself as "an irritable, impatient creature" by comparison. It was her job, she said, "to combat those things that excite my more sensitive temper … to control even this disposition whenever you think it improperly excited and to exert over me … the authority which it will be your privilege to use and my duty to yield to."

Then she added, "But do I speak of *duty*? You are of a too manly, too generous, too affectionate a disposition to like the word and God forbid I should ever be the wretched wife who obeyed her husband from a sense of duty alone." Her wedding ring, she told him, would not be "the badge of slavery, but the cherished link of the purest affection."

She was fiercely ambitious for him, and he became an extension of her own personality. She lived in her husband. When it was necessary she pushed and prodded him along in her subtle way.

She could never sit still. When, two years after their marriage, Franklin was given command of a ship in the Mediterranean, she plunged into a whirlwind of Middle Eastern travel through Greece, Egypt, Turkey, Syria, Asia Minor, and the Holy Land by cart and carriage, by ship and canal boat, on foot and on horseback.

When he returned to England in 1833, after his service in the Mediterranean, she was in Alexandria, preparing for a trip up the Nile. That didn't stop her from directing his career by long distance. She pushed him into going to see the First Lord of the Admiralty to ask for further employment.

He was told there was nothing available, whereupon she pushed him further. He had hoped to get a ship or a station with the Navy, but that wasn't good enough, she told him. What he should do was go to the Arctic again. Though she didn't want him to ruin his health, she pointed out, "A freezing climate seems to have a wonderful power of bracing your nerves and making you stronger."

She badly wanted him to go after the ultimate prize—the North West Passage. In that, she did not succeed. The Navy wasn't interested.

Franklin was offered a job as governor of Antigua, a tiny palm-fringed speck in the Caribbean. That was too much for Lady Franklin—an insulting comedown for an Arctic hero. It was a minor post, no more important than that of first lieutenant on a ship of the line. When a better offer came, that at least *sounded* better, the Franklins accepted it. He would be governor of Van Diemen's Land, a penal colony off the south coast of Australia.

That proved disastrous. John Franklin found himself the warden of a vast and horrible prison. In 1836 the colony consisted of more than seventeen thousand convicts and twenty-four thousand "free" citizens, many of them former convicts themselves. Each year another three thousand convicts arrived. It was a long way from the cold, clean air of the Arctic.

Franklin's six years there were the most painful in his life. He, and especially his wife, simply didn't fit in. They thought him a weakling and saw her as a meddler. She was the real problem. For she did not act the role of the ordinary governor's wife—dressing smartly, making and receiving calls, entertaining in public. Instead, she flung herself into her usual round of activity, visiting museums, prisons, and educational institutions.

That brought down a hail of criticism. She tried to look into the conditions endured by women convicts, and that didn't sit very well. She tried to start a college, but was stopped when the colonial secretary, Captain John Montague, insisted public money could not be wasted on such a project. "A more troublesome interfering woman I never saw," Montague said privately.

Instead of sitting quietly in Government House, she travelled about Australia, overland from Melbourne to Sydney by spring cart and horseback, for instance. She discussed everything, compiled statistics in her journals, and made herself unpopular.

In Franklin's view, and that of his wife, there was only one way he could regain that honour, and that was to perform some magnificent feat of exploration.

In Van Diemen's Land they considered her the power behind the throne. Her husband was called "a man in petticoats." He was no match for the powerful and wily civil servant, Montague, who engaged in a campaign against him that could have only one ending. When Franklin fired him, Montague through his friends in the press fought back, and travelled to England to lay his case before the colonial office.

Franklin received a stinging rebuke. His wife was now in a state of nervous collapse. The newspapers reported the explorer's replacement before he himself received official notice. And so, by 1844, he had reached the bottom of his career. More important, he felt his honour had been stained—and in nineteenth-century England, an Englishman's honour was all-important.

In Franklin's view, and that of his wife, there was only one way he could regain that honour, and that was to perform some magnificent feat of exploration. And so, once again, the North West Passage beckoned.

It is very doubtful if Franklin would have pushed so hard to go back to the Arctic if his reputation hadn't been at stake. He was, after all, in his sixtieth year, and that was an advanced age in which to face the Arctic blizzards. There were some who felt he was too old.

He wasn't only too old, he was also too plump. His friends worried about him if he didn't receive the posting. But others rallied to his cause. "If you don't let him go, the man will die of disappointment," was the way Sir Edward Parry, the other great Arctic explorer of his time, put it to the Navy.

In short, the most ambitious Arctic expedition yet mounted by Britain was to be led by a man who got the job because everybody felt sorry for him.

When Franklin set off, the Arctic Archipelago, as it was called—a maze of islands and channels—was still largely unknown. Franklin had found the narrow channel that ran along the North American coastline between the Beaufort Sea and King William Land. A parallel channel explored by Sir Edward Parry lay three hundred miles (480 km) to the north, leading from Baffin Bay to Viscount Melville Sound.

What lay in between was a blank on the map. It was believed that a connection could be made between the two channels, and the Navy, with its usual optimism, felt it could be conquered in a single two-month season. It was Franklin's job to try to find a way between the two.

His orders were to enter the Arctic through Lancaster Sound off Baffin Bay, and to sail straight on until he reached the great ice barrier near Viscount Melville Island. When he reached Cape Walker at the entrance to Melville Sound, he was to turn south or southwest and into unknown

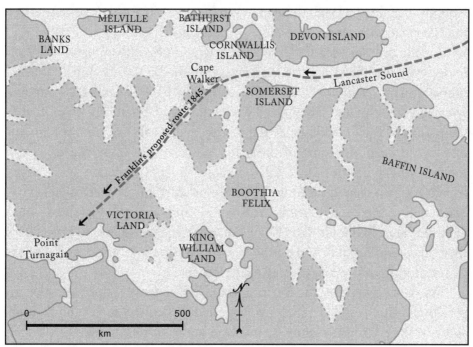

Franklin's proposed route from Cape Walker, 1845

waters to find the channel he had discovered along the Arctic coast. Having done that, he could proceed west along a fairly familiar coastline all the way to the Bering Sea.

But nobody could be sure of where he was going. There was a great blank space on the map—seventy thousand square miles (181,370 sq km) in size—through which he had been ordered to travel. Nobody knew what it contained. It might be a vast expanse of open ocean. It might be a larger land mass. Or it might be both.

In Franklin's instructions, somebody added an afterthought. If he couldn't go through to the south, then he was given permission to try a different route, north through the unexplored Wellington Channel. That unfortunate clause in his orders would be responsible for years of useless searching in the wrong direction.

Franklin would leave on two sailing ships with twenty-horsepower auxiliary engines, the first time engine power was used in the Arctic. He would have a crew of 134, and no one considered the problem of feeding them. Nobody explained why all these men were needed. The only reason was that the Navy had to keep its people busy in peacetime.

For the ordinary seaman, the voyage would often be a horror—at least in our eyes. But they were used to being crammed into tiny ships, squeezed into a swaying hammock at night, enduring back-breaking labour and wretched food by day. They faced long winters of boredom—confined to the prison of their cockleshells, the vessels themselves covered in a mantle of snow to keep out some of the cold. Alone in the Arctic wastes, out of touch with civilization for years, unable to communicate with wives, friends, or family, and faced with the almost certain prospect of scurvy—blackened gums, loose teeth, weariness, and mental fogginess—they endured. They had joined the Navy, not to see the world, but to provide for their families. They received double pay for Arctic exploration, and over the weary months and years, the pay mounted up.

Franklin's two ships, the *Erebus* and the *Terror*, were each larger than any previous Arctic vessel. That alone suggested difficulties in getting through some of the narrower channels, and over some of the known Arctic shallows. And incredibly, nobody had given a thought to the possibility that the expedition might encounter trouble.

Optimism reigned. Success, it was felt, was all but certain. No plans were made for a relief expedition—it would simply have been too costly. None of the people on board were hunters. Franklin intended to exist solely on his own provisions. Apparently he dismissed the threat of scurvy. Only one of his officers had any polar background. All these deficiencies were forgotten in the wave of enthusiasm that accompanied the Franklin expedition.

The president of the Royal Geographical Society was one of the optimists. "I have the fullest confidence that everything will be done for the promotion of science, and for the honour of the British name and Navy, that human efforts can accomplish," he exalted. "The name of Franklin alone is, indeed, a national guarantee ..."

And so, in the spring of 1845, the expedition set off. The two stubby little ships, gleaming in their fresh coats of black and yellow paint, were glimpsed by some Greenland whalers as they set off across Baffin Bay that summer. That was the last view the civilized world had of the *Erebus* and the *Terror* and their 129 men (five were sent home sick from Greenland). None was ever seen alive again.

CHAPTER THREE

The Great Search Begins

NO ONE KNOWS HOW FRANKLIN DIED, OR WHAT IT WAS THAT KILLED HIM. HIS BODY WAS NEVER FOUND. MEN IN SHIPS COMBED THE ARCTIC FOR TWELVE YEARS BEFORE THE FATE OF HIS EXPEDITION WAS UNRAVELLED. FOR ALL THAT TIME, ENGLISHMEN WAITED IN SUSPENSE.

Between 1848 and 1859, more than fifty expeditions were mounted to search for the aging explorer. Untold amounts of money were squandered. Ships sank, were lost or abandoned. Men died of mishap and scurvy. But when the great search finally came to an end, the white curtain of uncertainty had been drawn aside, the great archipelago of islands and channels had been charted, and the secret of the North West Passage—or as it turned out, *Passages*—had been unlocked. And yet a new century would dawn before anybody was able to take a ship through the Arctic from ocean to ocean.

The tale of the Franklin search is complicated and frustrating. Some of the men who took part were motivated as much by ambition as humanity. While searching for the lost ships, they were also seeking a greater prize— the elusive Passage. It needn't have taken twelve years. It didn't have to cost a sultan's ransom. It moved with maddening slowness. Franklin's fate could have been discovered as early as 1847, and some of his men could have been rescued. That didn't happen.

On the other hand, if the search hadn't taken place, the Arctic puzzle would have remained and most of that seventy-thousand-square-mile (181,370-sq-km) blank space on the map might easily have been explored and claimed by some other nation with the will or the funds to conduct the probe.

The search for Franklin allowed the British to claim ownership to most of the North American Arctic, which is now the Canadian Arctic. It made it possible for Canada to claim the Arctic as her own.

After two years passed with no word from Franklin, Jane Franklin began to have qualms. Returning from a whirlwind tour of travel from the West Indies to the United States, she was dismayed by the lack of news. Everybody had confidently assumed her husband would be dispatching letters home from the Bering Strait. None came. At this point some naval men were demanding that a search party go out.

But the Navy moved with a glacial slowness. In November 1847, with still no news from her husband and a third winter looming, she held a meeting at her home. And there she chose the explorer of the Antarctic, James Clark Ross, to lead any expedition to which the Admiralty might agree. It was clear at last that the Admiralty would agree to a search if Ross was in charge, because of his reputation.

No one except Lady Franklin was really concerned. In spite of the Admiralty's slow movement, optimism remained high. At the end of November, a local magazine interviewed a number of Arctic officers who insisted that Franklin had succeeded so well that he had already passed *through* Bering Strait and into the Pacific. But, in reality, by then Franklin had been dead nearly half a year, and his hungry crew, weakened by scurvy, were planning to abandon their icebound vessels.

> *Franklin's fate could have been discovered as early as 1847, and some of his men could have been rescued. That didn't happen.*

The Great Search began in 1848. The country was beginning to show concern over the fate of the expedition. In March, the first lord of the Admiralty announced a stupendous sum—twenty thousand pounds—would be paid to anybody who might help to save the lives of Franklin or his men. A later announcement offered half that sum to anyone who would merely discover what had really happened to the lost ships. That ten thousand pounds would be well over a million dollars in today's money.

The government planned an ambitious three-pronged attack that would see four ships, as well as an overland party, explore the maze of islands and channels from three directions, east, west, and south. Lady

Franklin herself was tempted to join one of these. She wrote to her missing husband—one of many letters that he never received—that "it would have been a less trial to me to come after you … but I thought of my duty & my interest to remain, for might I not have missed you … yet I've thought you to be ill, nothing should have stopped me …"

For eighteen months, while the three search expeditions were out of touch with the world, Jane Franklin waited in hope, persisting in the belief that her husband and his companions were still alive. She sent letters with every search party. James Ross had promised her he would be back in October of 1848, with Franklin and his ships. But October came and went with no word from any of the three expeditions. November found her, in her niece's words, "much out of health & in deep despondency." And the silence continued.

In January 1849, public prayers were being said in sixty churches for the safety of the expedition. Jane Franklin was committed heart and soul to the task of finding her missing husband. And she was employing every means to speed the search.

She went to English ports to interview whalers heading out for Baffin Bay, urging them to carry extra provisions in case they encountered the lost ships. She received a steady stream of callers in her London apartment—anybody who would tell her anything about the expedition, or make any suggestions. She even visited a mystic, who gave her the usual optimistic but inconclusive reading.

She launched into a campaign of letter writing that would have no end until the truth was known. She wrote Zachary Taylor, the new American president, appealing to his humanitarian and patriotic instincts. The president said he would do what he could.

The Admiralty, to whom she addressed another letter, was less enthusiastic. She wanted to borrow two ships and fit them out at her own expense. They refused. They sent a supply ship out after James Ross—that was enough for them. She wanted to go with it, but they refused to let her. She had to be content with another letter to her husband, who by this time had been dead for almost two years.

In the summer of 1849, she went to the Shetland and Orkney Islands in Scotland to interview more whalers who might have news of the missing men. They told her nothing. Two of the expeditions finally returned—including that of James Ross—and a kind of Arctic fever swept England. Books about polar journeys, dioramas showing Arctic vistas, newspaper and magazine articles about northern adventurers combined to increase the public interest.

But where was Franklin? Why hadn't he been found? How could two ships and 129 men vanish from sight without a word, without a hint, for almost five years? All of the expeditions returned empty-handed. Franklin seemed to have been swallowed up in the Arctic mists.

Now the Admiralty decided to send ships right around Cape Horn into the Pacific to enter the Arctic Ocean from the west. This was the first of *six* expeditions that would be sent off in 1850 to search for John Franklin.

The assumption was that Franklin had somehow got farther west. There was no basis for that belief, and it didn't sit well with Jane Franklin. She resolved to fit out her own expedition. The ships would have to be small, because she couldn't afford big ones. But she was confident she could raise money in the United States. She was determined her husband be found alive or dead. "There's no trial," she declared, "that I am not prepared to go through if it become necessary."

The idea of Franklin's lady squandering her last penny on a private quest didn't sit well with the English public, to whom she had become a heroine.

There were vast areas in the eastern Arctic, she knew, that had not been examined. Now she determined that these too would be searched.

She decided the Navy should hire a whaling captain, William Penny. At forty-one, he was the acknowledged leader of the Davis Strait whalers. He had been in the Arctic since the age of eleven, had commanded a whaling ship for sixteen years, and knew as much about the Arctic as anybody.

Penny was certainly not the Admiralty's choice. Whalers were not naval men, and the Admiralty wanted the British Navy and not the whalers to lead the search. But Jane Franklin moved behind the scenes to confirm him in this post.

She was prepared to pay for the expedition herself, if necessary, but was able to persuade the Admiralty to come up with the funds. The idea of Franklin's lady squandering her last penny on a private quest didn't sit well with the English public, to whom she had become a heroine. The Navy gave in.

Penny carried another letter to her lost husband. "I desire nothing," she wrote, "but to cherish the remainder of your days, however injured & broken your health may be … I live in you my dearest—I pray for you at all hours …"

At this point, May 1850, there were ten British ships heading for the Arctic searching for Franklin. In addition there were two American naval vessels, bringing the number of search vessels to an even dozen. That too was Lady Franklin's doing. She had persuaded Henry Grinnell, a New York philanthropist and shipping merchant, to underwrite the expedition.

Yet she remained uneasy. She was no longer an amateur where the Arctic was concerned. She had seen everybody, read everything, digested it all. Before the decade was out she would know more about the North than any armchair expert.

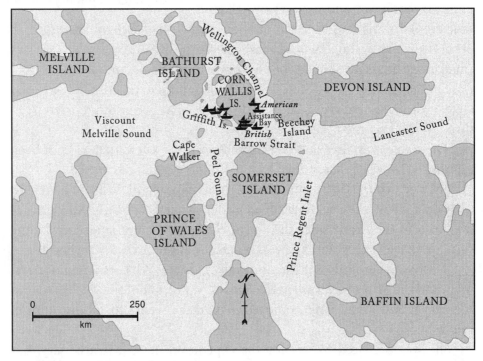

Area of the Franklin search, 1850–51

She suspected her husband's ships might have been caught on the ice—perhaps in James Ross Strait off King William Island. Perhaps they had abandoned their vessels and headed for the Great Fish River on the main continent. That was very close to what had actually happened, but Jane Franklin couldn't convince anybody of that possibility.

Expedition after expedition was setting off for the Arctic, but all were concentrating on the far North. The two American ships were heading for the very top of Baffin Bay. Penny was ordered to explore north of Lancaster Sound, but nobody apparently had considered looking at the coast to the south. And so Jane Franklin knew that she herself would have to see to that.

On June 5, her own modest expedition was ready to set off for that purpose in a ninety-ton (82-tonne) ship, the *Prince Albert*, a former pilot boat, outfitted with funds from other friends and her own dwindling fortune.

She herself drafted the orders. The commander, Lieutenant Charles Codrington Forsyth, a man with no Arctic experience, would proceed down Prince Regent Inlet to the narrowest part of Somerset Island, and then sledge south past the farthest point reached by James Ross. Had he been able to do that, he might have unlocked the riddle to the lost party.

Of all the thirteen ships searching the Arctic from the Bering Sea to Lancaster Sound, only this one was headed in the right direction. Few seemed to remember that John Franklin was a stubborn man with a reputation for following his orders to the letter. Those letters had been explicit. He was told to head west to Cape Walker (on the northern tip of Prince of Wales Island) and then head south. Only if the ice blocked his way was he to attempt another route north through the Wellington Channel. Lady Franklin was one of the few who believed it more than possible that her husband had found a way to stick to his original instructions. But then, she knew him better than any naval friend did.

CHAPTER FOUR

The First Clues

OF THE NINE SHIPS THAT LEFT ENGLAND IN 1850 TO PROBE THE EASTERN ARCTIC, ONLY ONE GOT BACK THAT YEAR. THE REST WERE IMPRISONED IN THE ICE OF BARROW STRAIT AND WELLINGTON CHANNEL AND, FROM THAT CENTRAL POINT, SLEDGING PARTIES SEARCHING FOR FRANKLIN FANNED OUT IN EVERY DIRECTION, EXCEPT THE RIGHT ONE.

The Arctic had never seen such activity, and would not see it again in that century. At last, the mysteries of that drab and silent realm were to be unlocked.

It was in this winter that some of the explorers found the first traces of the Franklin expedition. On a tiny little islet known as Beechey Island, off Devon Island at the mouth of the Wellington Channel, they discovered his first wintering spot.

Here were three mounds supported by three weathered headboards, marking the last resting place of a trio of Franklin's seamen, who had obviously died in the winter and early spring of 1846. As the party encountered more and more relics, there was no doubt now that this had been the main camp for the two wintering ships. Here were rope fragments, sail cloth, tarpaulins, casks, clothing, blankets, and scraps of paper strewn about. Here was a small mountain of six hundred empty preserved meat tins, filled with pebbles to form some sort of ballast. There was even a pair of officer's gloves laid out to dry on a rock.

But that only deepened the mystery. Franklin had left in a hurry apparently. He'd failed to leave any kind of memorandum or paper suggesting the direction he'd taken. He might have gone anywhere. For this Gibraltar-like island stood at the crossroads of the Arctic. Channels stretched off in every direction.

Then a few hints began to appear. Sledge tracks pointed north along the east coast of Wellington Channel. These were traced for forty miles (64 km). And so it looked to the searchers as if Franklin had explored the upper waters of the channel, preparing to examine it more thoroughly when spring came. This led to the guess—a mistaken one—that he'd headed north after all.

Meanwhile, back in England, Lady Franklin was preparing to launch another expedition. Forsyth had failed to get south of Prince Regent Inlet. She determined to try again with a new captain.

William Kennedy, a tough Canadian fur trader, the son of a Cree woman and Hudson's Bay factor, volunteered even though he had never been to sea in his life. His second-in-command would be Joseph-René Bellot, a twenty-five-year-old French naval officer. He too knew nothing about the Arctic, except what he had read in books.

What they lacked in experience, this odd pair made up for in enthusiasm. Both volunteered to serve Lady Franklin's cause without fee. They came to London of their own accord and at their own expense to answer her call for help—two outsiders from alien worlds with no link to any of the several British establishments involved in the search for her husband.

Jane Franklin was by now an international heroine. She was impressed by Kennedy, who had abandoned his business and, over the protests of his family, hurried to her side. And she was stimulated by Bellot's youthful ardour. Indeed, she treated him as if he were her son.

The Admiralty wasn't so enthusiastic. The idea of a naval officer from a foreign country serving under an untutored mixed-blood from the wilds of sub-Arctic America was to them madness.

But Lady Franklin won out. After all, it was she and not the Navy who was paying for the voyage. Actually, the voyage that followed, though arduous, was one of the happiest in Arctic history.

By the fall of 1851, all but one of the ships sent to the eastern Arctic were home. Only Kennedy's was still out in the polar wilderness. Once more Jane Franklin was in despair. The discovery of John Franklin's wintering place at Beechey Island had only increased the mystery. Where on earth had he gone in the following spring of 1846? Had both vessels sunk with all hands? In all the history of Arctic exploration that had never happened. Had he been forced to change his original route? If so, why hadn't he left cairns to mark his passage?

Every effort had been made to communicate with the missing expedition. Sailors had painted or chalked gigantic messages on the cliffs. Ships had left caches of food and clothing. Foxes had been trapped and released wearing collars carrying messages in the unlikely event that some of Franklin's men might shoot them for food. Balloons were sent off with papers carrying information about the location of the rescue ships. Blue lights were flashed, guns fired, rockets exploded in the Arctic night. But the Arctic remained silent.

Apart from an unexplained scrap of British elm found by Penny off Wellington Channel, only one other clue had appeared, and it too was not identified. This was two fragments of wood that had clearly been part of a Royal Navy vessel, picked up on the south coasts of Wollaston and Victoria Land by John Rae, of the Hudson's Bay Company. Years had passed before anyone realized they were almost certainly from one of Franklin's ships.

The country grasped at straws, clinging to the belief that the lost crews might still be alive, and so did Lady Franklin. She and her friend, Sophia Cracroft, bombarded the press with anonymous letters and the Admiralty with signed petitions urging more action.

That fall, besides Kennedy in the eastern Arctic, only two other search ships remained—both in the west. And nobody knew exactly where they were. The Navy's major expeditions had been branded as a failure, and the Navy was reluctant to start any more.

There was one bright spot—public opinion was still on Jane Franklin's side. The *Times* called for a complete review of the Franklin search and insisted on knowing the government's plans for the future. It urged "a little more continuous perseverance." Her campaign was bearing fruit.

All the old Arctic hands were convinced, as were the public and press, that Franklin had gone north and vanished somewhere up the Wellington Channel. That is where everybody felt the search should continue.

In the spring of 1852, the Navy gave in to the pressure. It promised to send *five* ships this time, under a crusty old naval hand, Sir Edward Belcher. His orders were to look for the lost explorer somewhere to the north of Beechey Island. In short, in the wrong direction.

By the spring of 1852, it seemed to Lady Franklin that every corner of the Great Archipelago would be scrutinized. Nine ships were in the Arctic—one well to the north, five in the centre, two more somewhere in the west north of Alaska. And her own sloop, the *Prince Albert* under William Kennedy, was presumably searching the southern maze of channels. Everything that could be done had been done, or so it seemed. Surely before another year was out, the mystery would be solved.

BOOTHIA
PENINSULA

KING
WILLIAM
ISLAND

CHAPTER FIVE

One Final Gamble

UNKNOWN TO LADY FRANKLIN, IN FEBRUARY OF 1852, KENNEDY AND
BELLOT SET OFF ON THE LONGEST SLEDGE JOURNEY IN ARCTIC HISTORY—
1,265 MILES (2,036 KM) IN NINETY-FIVE DAYS. BUT THEY HAD FOUND NO
TRACE OF FRANKLIN.

They traced a great clockwise circle, down Prince Regent Inlet, across
Somerset Island and Peel Sound, up to Prince of Wales Island, and north to
Cape Walker. Then they moved east along Barrow Strait to Port Leopold,
and back to where their ships were anchored in Batty Bay on the eastern
shore of Somerset Island.

Alas, they didn't go as far south as the region of the North Magnetic
Pole, off King William Land, as Lady Franklin had ordered. Perhaps this was
because Kennedy was suffering from snow blindness, and perhaps also
because both men thought they saw a land barrier blocking Peel Sound.
Thus they assumed that Franklin could not have come that way.

It would have been more profitable if Kennedy had listened to Bellot,
who wanted to go to the bottom of Prince Regent Inlet and talk to the
Inuit there. He reasoned that if more than a hundred men were lost in the
area, the Inuit would at least have heard of it. He was right, but he gave in
to Kennedy.

Meanwhile, at least two search vessels were missing—and seemed to be
lost. These were the two ships sent out to explore the western Arctic under
Captain William Collinson and Captain Robert McClure. And so new
search parties were sent out to look for the searchers.

Actually the two ships had become separated. McClure was frozen in at
Mercy Bay on Banks Island, his crew close to starvation. Collinson was farther south. McClure, indeed, had discovered the North West Passage—or

one of them—and was eventually rescued by some of Belcher's party who brought him overland from Mercy Bay to Beechey Island. He had, therefore, gone all the way from west to east—but not entirely by ship. Much of the journey had been made by sledge, and so although the Passage had been discovered, it had not yet been navigated.

As for Belcher's five-ship expedition, it ended in total confusion. To everybody's astonishment and disgust, Belcher actually abandoned four ships in the Arctic, all in good condition, and none in any real danger of being trapped for a second winter.

An aging and cranky commander, he had no intention of spending another season in the Arctic, and so committed the worst blunder of the entire search. This "last of the Arctic voyages," as Belcher was to call it, was also, apart from the Franklin loss, the most disastrous. The mystery had not been solved. Captain Collinson and his missing vessel had been callously forsaken, and four big naval ships, all in perfect condition, abandoned. Sir Edward Belcher became the laughing stock of the Royal Navy.

On January 12, 1854, Jane Franklin got the first of several shocks. The Admiralty, without waiting for Belcher or any others to return, announced that as of March 31, the names of all the officers and crew members of the *Erebus* and the *Terror* would be struck from its books.

She was stunned. She already had the first news of McClure's discovery of the North West Passage. Was that all that counted? Her husband's fate was still unknown. There were a few who held out the hope he or some of his crew were still alive among the Inuit. She was one of these, but now it seemed as if the long quest for the Arctic hero had been a sham—an excuse to seek not human beings, but the elusive Passage.

She wrote an indignant letter to the Admiralty. She called the Navy's decision "presumptuous in the sight of God." In a bold act of defiance, she refused to wear black mourning, and appeared in brilliant pink and green. That was to show she hadn't given up hope.

Four days before her husband was officially declared dead, the Crimean War broke out between Russia on one side and Turkey, England, and France on the other. The Navy couldn't afford the luxury of any more Arctic searches. Every ship would be needed in the struggle against the Russians.

With Belcher's return in the late fall, the Admiralty lost all stomach for polar exploration. In just two years, six ships had been abandoned, or lost. Why waste any more money on a wild goose chase? Jane Franklin could argue that the fate of her husband and crew were still unknown. But even that point was lost when the Hudson's Bay's explorer, John Rae, arrived in England with the first firm news.

At Pelly Bay, on April 21, 1854, an Inuit told a fascinating tale—one that would be worth ten thousand pounds to Rae and his men. He'd heard stories from other Natives of thirty-five or forty whites who had starved to death some years before, west of a large river, perhaps ten or twelve days' journey away. Later, the Natives brought a treasure trove of relics to him, easily identified as having belonged to Franklin and his men—silver forks and spoons, marked with officers' crests, one of Franklin's medals, a small plate bearing his name, and other relics, including a gold watch, a surgeon's knife, and a silver pencil case.

When Lady Franklin learned, in the spring of 1856, that Rae had succeeded in his claim for the ten-thousand-pound reward offered for finding some clues to her husband's fate, she was irritated and dismayed. It was far too early, she said, to come to any conclusion as to what had happened. Rae's prize might confirm the government's belief that her husband was dead, but she couldn't bring herself to accept that.

She attacked the Admiralty again, "though it is my humble hope and fervent prayer that the Government of my country will themselves complete the work they have done and not leave it to a weak and helpless woman to attempt the doing that imperfectly which they themselves can do so easily and well, yet, if need be, such is my painful resolve, God helping me."

Of course, she was anything but weak and helpless. She was iron-willed and had the support of some of the most powerful figures in the country, not the least of whom was Prince Albert, the husband of the queen. She was a formidable public figure, having captured the imagination and appealed to the chivalry of the ordinary Briton, who saw her, indeed, as a weak and helpless woman, battling for her husband's life and honour. Almost single-handedly she had created a myth, turning John Franklin, a likeable, but quite ordinary naval officer, into *the* Arctic hero.

No explorer was ever as obsessed as Jane Franklin. She could not let go.

Her obsession sustained her, giving her life a meaning and a focus. Her Pall Mall residence in London was nicknamed The Battery, because she had battered the Admiralty with so many letters and memorials. And when she wasn't battering against the walls of officialdom, or writing to foreign powers, or penning letters to the *Times*, thinly disguised under false names, she was influencing events from behind the scenes.

It was Lady Franklin who persuaded thirty-six of London's leading men of science, including all the major Arctic explorers, to send a memorial to the prime minister, suggesting that some of Franklin's men were still alive among the Inuit, and urging further action.

She kept up the public barrage the following year, while her allies worked for her in Parliament. She had appealed to the prime minister the previous December, and now that lengthy letter, which ran to more than three thousand words, was circulated in pamphlet form. It announced she was prepared to sacrifice her entire available fortune to pay the cost of a private expedition, if the government didn't budge.

At the same time she managed to arrange for a group of Americans to back her case with the Admiralty. It had little effect. But she would not be stopped. She had her eye on a steam yacht in Aberdeen, the *Fox*. She bought it for two thousand pounds and persuaded an old Arctic hand, Leopold M'Clintock, to take it to the Arctic to King William Island—the one spot that nobody had yet searched. There, she was certain, the secret of her husband's fate would be unravelled.

The Admiralty offered some help in the form of provisions. And M'Clintock offered to captain the ship at no cost to Lady Franklin. This was a small schooner-rigged steam yacht of 170 tons (154 tonnes), half the size of one of Franklin's vessels.

It had only made one voyage—to Norway. The quarters for the ship's company of twenty-five (seventeen of whom had taken part in previous Franklin searches) were incredibly cramped. The officers were "crammed into pigeon holes" to make room for provisions and stores. The room in which five persons ate was only eight feet (2.4 m) square. A few small coal stoves replaced the standard heating apparatus.

But M'Clintock, who had been moved by the wave of public sympathy that swept the country when his expedition was announced, confirmed the impression that "the glorious mission entrusted to me was in reality, *a great national duty.*"

He refused to take a single penny from Lady Franklin. The other commissioned officers followed suit. Allen Young, his sailing master, not only served without pay, but also donated five hundred pounds to the public subscription that was rapidly approaching the three-thousand-pound mark. All the same, Jane Franklin would still have to dip into her own funds for an additional seven thousand.

And so, on the last day of June, 1847, before the ship sailed from the Orkneys for Greenland, she came down to Aberdeen to bid him goodbye. He could see how deeply agitated she was when she left the yacht. He tried without success to prevent the crew from giving her the usual three lusty cheers. Public demonstrations of that kind embarrassed her. They cheered anyway, and for that, M'Clintock was grateful.

And so the *Fox* set off on the last expedition to search for John Franklin. Twelve years had gone by since Franklin set out to find the Passage. And now the final voyage of that long search to discover his fate had been dispatched.

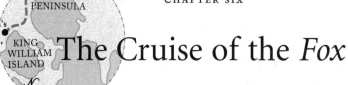

CHAPTER SIX

The Cruise of the *Fox*

THE *FOX* HEADED OUT INTO THE ATLANTIC. AT THIS POINT M'CLINTOCK READ
TO THE CREW A LETTER LADY FRANKLIN HAD GIVEN HIM BEFORE HE LEFT,
REMINDING HIM THAT THE EXPEDITION HAD THREE PURPOSES. THESE WERE:
FIRST, AND MOST IMPORTANT, THE RESCUE OF THE SURVIVORS; SECOND, THE
RECOVERY OF "THE UNSPEAKABLY PRECIOUS DOCUMENTS OF THE EXPEDITION";
AND THIRD, THE PROOF OF HER OWN CLAIMS, THAT "THESE MARTYRS IN A NOBLE
CAUSE ACHIEVED AT THEIR LAST EXTREMITY" THE DISCOVERY OF THE NORTH
WEST PASSAGE.

"My only fear," Jane Franklin wrote, "is that you may spend yourselves
too much in the effort; and you must therefore let me tell you how much
dearer to me even than any of them is the preservation of the valuable lives
of the little band of heroes who are your companions and followers."

And so, the final voyage had begun. "I am doomed to trial & to struggle
on to the end," Jane Franklin had written a year before. That struggle was
continuing. But at last the end was in sight.

That was her triumph. This remarkable Victorian gentlewoman had
inspired a loyalty that queens might envy and, through her persistence,
added a footnote to history. As one newspaper wrote, "What the nation
would not do, a woman did."

The *Fox* reached Upernavik on the western coast of Greenland on
August 6, 1857. M'Clintock had hoped to push westward, straight to the
main ice pack in Baffin Bay, but the ice was too much for him. His only
chance was to try to get around it by heading north and circling before
coming south again. To do that he would have to cut directly across the
shallow crescent of Melville Bay. That was the most feared stretch of open
water on the Greenland coast. To his dismay, he found that conditions there
were the worst on record.

He managed to push his ship three-quarters of the way across, before he was blocked. But M'Clintock never lost his cool. If his ship was trapped in ice, well then, he would wait until the next year and do it again.

Yet he had to be concerned. The crew did not know what was going on. But he did. He was faced with eight lonely winter months trapped in the ice pack.

That was bad enough. The danger of being crushed was worse. The *Fox* wasn't powerful enough to push the ice floes apart. All attempts to blast it free failed. By September he'd lost control of his ship. He decided to make the best of it.

He organized a school, unpacked an organ, and taught his men to build snow houses on the ice. Two Inuit hunters in the party brought in seals and an occasional bear. Meanwhile, the ice pushed the ship farther and farther south—farther and farther away from their goal. By April 26, they had been caught on the ice for 250 days and they had travelled 1,385 miles (2,230 km), most of it in the wrong direction.

At times the Fox shuddered so violently that ship's bells rang and crewmen were almost knocked off their feet.

The ice began to break, and a scene of terror followed. The ship rolled wickedly in the heavy seas, bruised and buffeted by the ice floes. M'Clintock knew that a single blow by one of those monster ice blocks could crush his ship in an instant. At times the *Fox* shuddered so violently that ship's bells rang and crewmen were almost knocked off their feet.

"Such a battering ... I hope not to see again," M'Clintock wrote, describing one eighteen-hour period of torment. He knew then, he said, why a man's hair could turn grey in a few hours.

Then suddenly it was over. The ice was gone. They were free. M'Clintock could have gone south into harbour at St. John's, Newfoundland, to repair his ship and take on extra food. He didn't. Instead he went right back up the coast of Greenland and across Melville Bay, fighting his way once again through the ice.

Finally he reached the mouth of Lancaster Sound—the only real entrance into the Arctic maze. He used up most of his coal fighting his way through the ice, but he found more in a depot that Belcher had left at

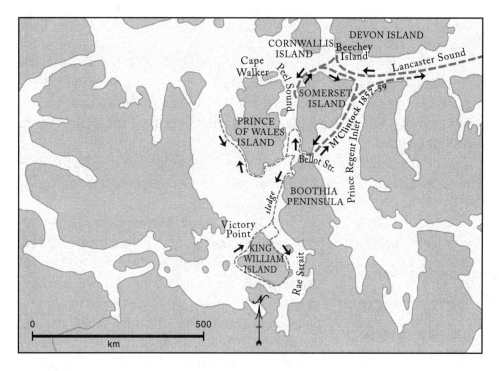

M'Clintock's expedition to King William Island, 1857–59

Beechey Island, Franklin's first wintering place. And from that point the real voyage began.

M'Clintock realized that Franklin must have gone south down Peel Sound to the west of Somerset, in spite of what the early explorers had said about the ice barring the way. That was the only route that hadn't been thoroughly explored. He could see Cape Walker in the distance at the northern tip of Prince of Wales Island. Franklin had been ordered to go south of the Cape. And so M'Clintock followed in his track, "in a wild state of excitement—a mingling of anxious hopes and fears!"

After twenty-five miles, a dike of ice barred his way. There wasn't a moment to lose. He turned about and chose another route.

He decided to go down Prince Regent Inlet and then try to slip back in to Peel Sound by way of a narrow passage named for Bellot. He pushed the *Fox* westward through Bellot Strait and was halfway through before he knew it. Now all he had to do was wait at the mouth of the strait until the ice vanished. He had no choice anyway. A stiff current drove the *Fox* help-lessly back "almost capsizing it."

M'Clintock was convinced that this little strait was the link to the North West Passage. It was only twenty miles (32 km) long and scarcely a mile (1.6 km) wide at its narrowest point. Once they were through it, they were in easy reach of King William Island, which he knew held the answer to the Franklin mystery.

But this was not to be. They tried six times to get through Bellot Strait and were driven back each time by the ice. And so they were forced to anchor for the winter in a sheltering inlet at the eastern end.

One had seen the bones of a white man, who'd died on an island in the river many years before—probably Montreal Island in the delta of the Great Fish River on the main coast of North America.

M'Clintock planned three major sledge expeditions that winter. And this time they would use some dogs. This most efficient form of Arctic travel, which the Inuit had long known, had been rejected by the Navy, which preferred to put men in harness. In addition, M'Clintock was prepared to save the extra weight of tents by building snow houses. He was learning from the Inuit at last.

On a scouting trip, down the west coast of Boothia Peninsula, he encountered a group of four Inuit. These were the first Natives they had run into. M'Clintock noticed that one was wearing a naval button. They told him it had come from some white men who had starved on an island and a river. One of the Inuit had been to the island and brought back some wood and iron.

M'Clintock offered to trade presents for information and relics. A day or so later, an entire village of forty-five arrived—men, women, and children. M'Clintock was able to bring to the *Fox* a quantity of silver cutlery, a medal, part of a gold chain, several buttons, and knives, fashioned by the Natives out of wood and iron, obviously from the wrecked ship.

But none had seen any of Franklin's lost crew. One had seen the bones of a white man, who'd died on an island in the river many years before—probably Montreal Island in the delta of the Great Fish River on the main coast of North America. One or two remembered a ship crushed by the ice, to the west of King William Island. They said the vessel had sunk, but the crew had got off safely. Thus the vague outlines of the Franklin tragedy began to emerge.

M'Clintock set off again south on April 2. He met more Inuit that told him of two ships—one had sunk, the other had been forced ashore badly damaged. White men had been seen, they told him, hauling boats south toward a large river on the mainland.

Then, on a frozen channel between Boothia Peninsula and King William Island, M'Clintock came upon a village whose inhabitants had more Franklin relics, including a silver plate, bearing the crests of the explorer and his first officer, and other members of the expedition.

There were more hints of the lost party: tales of the wreck of a ship without masts, of books strewn across the Arctic wastes, of white men who dropped in their tracks on the way to the Great Fish River, some of whom were buried, and some not.

M'Clintock met an old woman and a boy who'd been the last to visit the wrecked ship, apparently during the winter of 1857-58. But the dates were vague and much of the information second-hand.

M'Clintock moved south along the island's eastern coastline and encountered more Inuit. In that treeless land, wood was more precious than gold. They'd made kayak paddles, snow shovels, spear handles, tent poles, and a variety of objects from wood they'd got from other Inuit. Obviously it had been scavenged from a ship, but none of these people knew anything about white men who had died on their shores.

M'Clintock knew his task would not be easy. The Natives had plundered everything they could find, throwing away what they didn't need—such as books and papers—adapting the rest for their own use. And a ghostly shroud of snow still covered the land, hiding the remains of the lost men.

It was all very frustrating. M'Clintock kept on south to Montreal Island on the Great Fish Delta, haunted by the shades of men long dead. Here, he and his party found a bit of a preserved meat tin, and some scraps of iron and copper. These too were second-hand relics. A Native stone marker made it clear that this was plunder taken earlier and set aside for later. In the eerie silence of the Arctic spring, M'Clintock circled the bleak and rugged coastline of Montreal Island by dog team. But he found no evidence that any of Franklin's crew had got that far.

He turned back on May 24 to King William Island, travelling along the sea ice that overlapped the shore. Driving his own team, he kept a sharp lookout. Again, snow shrouded the beach. At midnight, with the sun still bright in the sky, he trudged along a gravel ridge that had been swept clean, and there, with dramatic suddenness, he came upon a human skeleton.

This was a major find—the only first-hand evidence anybody had yet had of the Franklin disaster. There it lay, a grisly witness to history, the body face down, as if the owner had stumbled forward and dropped, never to move again. The bones were as white as chalk. A few rags clung to them. The limbs bore signs of having been gnawed at by animals.

He'd been a young man, slight, probably a steward, or an officer's servant. He hadn't been warmly clad. A clothes brush and a pocket comb lay close by. Gazing down on his grim find, M'Clintock remembered what an old Inuit woman had said to him: "They fell down and died as they walked along."

Up the gloomy and desolate west coast of the island, M'Clintock's party moved. He was sure that Franklin's men must have left some sort of record. But if they had, the Inuit had scattered it to the winds. If only the Navy had been quicker in its rescue operations, if the old Arctic hands hadn't been so short-sighted, if Lady Franklin's own ships had only kept going, the full story of Franklin's fate would undoubtedly have been discovered. At this late date, finding it seemed hopeless.

And then, farther up the coast, he came upon a cairn, built by another of his sledging parties, containing a message. One of his lieutenants, William Hobson, had been there six days before. He had seen nothing of a wrecked ship. He'd met no Natives. But he *had* found a document! In a cairn at Victory Point on the northwestern shore of King William Island, he discovered the only record ever found of the lost Franklin expedition. It wasn't much, but it was enough to clear up the main points of the mystery.

CHAPTER SEVEN

Solving the Mystery

THE DOCUMENT FOUND AT VICTORY POINT PROVIDED THE ONLY FIRST-HAND INFORMATION EVER UNCOVERED ABOUT THE PROGRESS AND FATE OF THE MISSING CREWS. ACTUALLY, THERE WERE TWO MESSAGES — TWO CRAMPED SCRIBBLES WRITTEN A YEAR APART IN THE MARGINS OF A REGULAR ADMIRALTY FORM.

The first message was dated May 28, 1847, and was signed by Lieutenant G. M. Gore. It was cheerful enough: "All well," it read. It revealed that Franklin had certainly gone up the Wellington Channel and had, in fact, circled round before settling down at Beechey Island for the winter of 1845–46.

It also revealed that he had been caught on the ice stream just west of the northern tip of King William Island during his second winter in the Arctic. Gore and his party of seven were fully confident the two ships would be freed that summer and the Passage discovered.

But that was wishful thinking as the second message made clear. Written in a different hand and signed by Franklin's two deputies, Lieutenant Francis Crozier, and Lieutenant James Fitzjames, it was dated April 27, 1848, and told a gloomier story.

Franklin had died the previous June, only a month after Gore had scribbled his first message. At the time of the second message, the ships had been trapped on the ice for nineteen months. No fewer than nine officers (including Gore) and fifteen men were dead. The rest had left the two vessels and were trying to reach the Great Fish River. Now there was enough to piece together the probable story of the last expedition of Sir John Franklin.

Racing to make time before the onset of autumn weather in 1845, Franklin apparently didn't stop to build cairns or leave letters. With sails full out, he pressed confidently on to the open waters of Lancaster Sound. After all, the eternal optimist expected to be sailing into the North Pacific in less than a year—why leave a message?

He pushed on through Barrow Strait. Somewhere ahead loomed the cliffs of Cape Walker, the last known point of land. To the southwest lay the Unknown, which his instructions had ordered him to explore.

But he found that direction blocked by ice. On the western shore of Devon Island he could see a stretch of clear water—Wellington Channel. And so, following his instructions, he made for this alternate route and sailed north into unexplored territory. Was it a strait, or merely a bay? No map could tell him.

The two ships headed north until the presence of an unnamed and unexplored peninsula (now the Grinnell Peninsula) forced them to the northwest. At the very tip of the peninsula, Franklin once again found his way barred by a wall of ice.

He was forced to go back south through a different channel. Now he realized he'd rounded Cornwallis Land, which was actually an island. He went back into Barrow Strait north of Cape Walker and was again frustrated in his attempt to push west. But directly to the south he found another channel, and he knew that beyond that, somewhere in the area of King William Land, the way was clear to the western sea. Earlier explorers had discovered that.

It was obviously too late to make the attempt that year. He'd have to find a safe anchorage. And so he made for Beechey Island and spent the winter there, where three of his men died of natural causes—not an unusual number—and were buried on the spot. (Almost 150 years later, these bodies were exhumed, and it was discovered that the men had died from a combination of tuberculosis and perhaps lead poisoning).

Now he was within 350 miles (563 km) of his goal. Once the gap between Beechey Island and King William Land was closed, he would be near familiar waters leading west. Why didn't he leave a note for others to find? He spent the entire winter there. He was equipped for the usual activities—amateur theatricals, target practice, scientific observations, the collection of specimens. Yet no one, apparently, thought to leave a single scrap of paper outlining the expedition's plans for the following summer.

That is the mystery surrounding the tragedy. It raises questions that

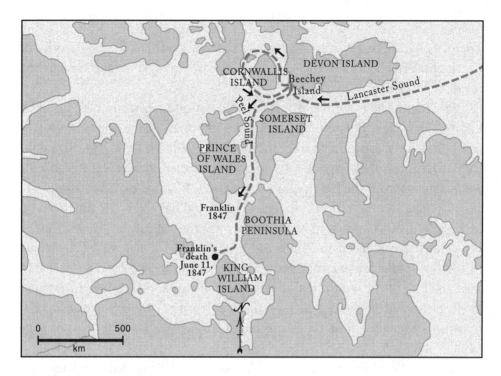

Franklin's last expedition, 1845–47

cannot be answered. Was it because the optimistic explorer was so certain of getting through that he really didn't think it necessary? Was it because the two ships were driven away from Beechey along the ice in a sudden spring gale, before he had time to prepare a record? Or did he actually leave a message that was never found? No one knows.

What is known is that he followed orders and set his course that spring for the south. He didn't realize he was sailing directly toward the great ice stream that pours down from the Beaufort Sea. Driven by the winds from the northwest, this mighty frozen river, frightening in its power, squeezes its way between the bleak islands, as it seeks warmer waters. It is like a floating glacier, up to one-hundred-feet (30-m) thick, unbroken by any channel. It forms a slow moving wall of ice that nobody can penetrate.

Flowing down between Melville and Banks Islands and through Melville Sound, the ice stream forces itself against the western shores of Prince of Wales Island. Then it curves down the unexplored channel on the eastern side of Victoria Land to block the narrows at King William Land. There its southern edge encounters the warmer waters flowing from the continental rivers and begins to break apart, leaving the channels to the south fairly clear.

Faced with the presence of this vast, slow moving frozen mass, Franklin had to turn back. But another unknown channel, Peel Sound, lay to the south. It too beckoned in the direction of King William Land. He turned his ships south into these mysterious waters. It seemed to be clear because he was sheltered from the ice stream by the bulk of Prince of Wales Island.

When he emerged from Peel Sound he would have seen the northern tip of King William Land dead ahead—only a hundred miles (160 km) away. But once he emerged from the protecting shield of Prince of Wales Island he would again have encountered the ice stream. To stay clear of that he'd have to cling to the west coast of Boothia Peninsula. But sooner or later he knew he would be forced to face the ice, because the only route to the known Passage shown on the maps led directly down the west coast of King William Land.

In 1846, Franklin had no way of knowing that King William Land was an island. He could have got away from the ice stream by cutting around the island's eastern side and slipping down the narrow strait that separates it from the main coast of North America. But Franklin would have thought this was a dead end, since he believed King William Land was a peninsula.

And so he turned his ships into the ice stream and winter closed in. On September 12, 1846, the *Erebus* and the *Terror* were imprisoned in the frozen river that moved south at the agonizingly slow speed of one and one-half miles (2.4 km) a month.

The explorer died the following June. The mystery of his death has never been solved, nor has his burial place ever been found. He was almost certainly buried at sea, but we don't know what caused his sudden passing. All was well when Gore scribbled that first message. A year later, as a second message made clear, Franklin was gone and Lieutenant Crozier was in command. All we know is that Franklin was not healthy and was in his sixtieth year. He was obviously too old to undertake such a quest—the victim of his friends' sentiment, the Navy's rigidity, his own optimism, and his wife's ambition.

The fate of his men is less mysterious. Over the years more skeletons and fragments of skeletons have been discovered. Modern research has shown evidence of cannibalism, scurvy, and lead poisoning from the poorly soldered tins of meat. The Inuit description of the crews' final stages suggests that most died from scurvy—the disease that haunted almost every Arctic expedition. Scurvy can be cured by fresh vegetables, fresh fruits, and also fresh meat, as the Inuit well knew. But the two Franklin ships were heavily stocked with salt meat. That contributed to their fate.

The story was a familiar one, as the messages at Victory Point suggested. All was well one year; twenty-four men were dead the next. And with the men dying daily in the following winter, Crozier knew his only hope lay in abandoning the ship before the entire company perished.

For the *Erebus* and the *Terror*, there was no way out of the floating trap. It had been the coldest winter in living memory. The ice hadn't melted. Its progress was too slow.

Crozier's mistake was to head south to the Great Fish River. Perhaps he thought that a relief party might have been sent there. If so, he underestimated the slowness of the British Admiralty, and the foolish optimism of the Arctic Council of Polar Experts, who showed little concern about Franklin, and didn't move until the spring of 1848, when the surviving crews were already sledging to their deaths.

It would have been impossible for Crozier's weakened men to navigate the many cataracts of the Great Fish River even if they'd reached it. Up the coast of Prince Regent Sound lay a cache of goods and provisions dumped there by a previous expedition. But it's doubtful if they could have reached that either, since they neither had dogs nor dog drivers, and the sledges were too heavy and cumbersome to move swiftly.

M'Clintock came upon one of these Navy sledges not far beyond the rugged cape he named for Captain Crozier. What he saw shocked him. The sledge itself was a monstrous contraption of iron and oak, weighing at least 650 pounds (295 kg). On top of it was a twenty-eight-foot (8.5-m) boat rigged for river travel weighing another seven or eight hundred pounds (317-362 kg). To M'Clintock, this was madness. Seven healthy men would have had trouble hauling it any distance, even if it hadn't been loaded.

But it *was* loaded—with an incredible stock of useless articles. Here were books, every kind of footgear, towels and toothbrushes, gun covers and twine, soap and sheet lead, dinner knives, crested silver plate, pocket watches and tools, a bead purse, a cigar case—everything, in short, that the civilized traveller considered necessary for his comfort and well-being. But as M'Clintock wrote, it was for a sledge traveller of those times "a mere accumulation of dead weight …"

Inside he found eerie evidence of this truth. Here were sprawled two skeletons—one of a slight young man, the other of an older and sturdier seaman. They'd got this far and no farther. While their comrades had abandoned most of their supplies and struggled on, they had been left behind.

M'Clintock was convinced they were returning to the ship for more provisions. But the ship was at least sixty-five miles (105 km) to the north. Unable to drag their boat farther, they'd left the two weakest of their number with a little food, some tea and chocolate, expecting perhaps to return with fresh stock. Scurvy, which weakens the muscles, also clouds the mind, making its victims believe they can accomplish more than they are able to.

At Victory Point where the cairn containing the message was found, there was another extraordinary pile of goods. This was further proof that the men who abandoned the ships weren't aware of the extent to which they had been weakened. They piled their sledges with ten tons (9 tonnes) of gear and abandoned most of it three days later when they reached Victory Point.

The huge heap of discarded woollen clothing was four feet (1.2 m) high. But they'd also brought along button polish, heavy cookstoves, brass curtain rods, a lightning conductor, and a library of religious books. Why? It had taken them three days to haul this enormous quantity of useless articles fifteen miles (24 km), before they realized they couldn't go farther. And so, after thawing out some ink and scribbling the second note, they lightened their sledges and headed south to their deaths.

M'Clintock left this gloomy scene on June 2, and was back on the *Fox* on June 19. No other trace of Franklin had been found, except on King William Island. But together, three sledge expeditions from the *Fox* had charted eight hundred miles (1,287 km) of new coastline. So that, by now, almost all that part of the Arctic Archipelago had been unveiled as a result of the long, blundering search for Franklin.

That was a supreme irony of the quest for the North West Passage. The Passage itself would have little commercial value, even with the development of modern icebreakers. It was a symbol to gain public support for geographical and scientific investigation. And a symbol it remained.

Had Franklin been able to make his way through it, further exploration would have been postponed, probably for decades. The continued bungling of the Navy kept the flame alive and prolonged the explorations, and that was partially due to Lady Franklin's continual campaign. It had cost a great deal of money and taken a long time and caused the deaths of several men, but it wasn't entirely wasted. By the time M'Clintock returned to England, in September of 1859, most of the southern Arctic had been mapped.

CHAPTER EIGHT

The Sainthood of John Franklin

LADY FRANKLIN WAITED RESTLESSLY FOR M'CLINTOCK'S RETURN. BUT SHE COULD NOT STAY STILL. SO OFF SHE WENT, WITH HER NIECE SOPHIA, ON ANOTHER OF THOSE EXHAUSTING JOURNEYS THAT MARKED HER CAREER. SHE SAID SHE DID IT TO STRENGTHEN HERSELF FOR THE POSSIBLE SOLUTION OF THE LONG DRAMA, WHICH SHE HOPED M'CLINTOCK WOULD UNVEIL.

What if he failed? How much longer could she continue the struggle to reclaim her husband's honour? How many more expeditions might be needed? And how many more could she afford to finance? There was so little time.

On her sixtieth birthday she had scribbled: "I cannot write down all the feelings that press upon me now as I think how fast the sands of life are ebbing away." But this was premature. In 1858, six years after she wrote those words, while M'Clintock was enduring the freeze-up in Bellot Strait, she determined to set off once more. She wouldn't go on foot this time because she was suffering from phlebitis. She would travel by boat and train through France, Greece, the Crimean battlefields, and North Africa.

Everybody knew her; everybody met her. In Athens she had an audience with the Queen of Greece, in Tunis with the Bey himself and his prime minister in the privacy of his harem, which, out of feminine curiosity, she asked to see.

She had not returned to London when M'Clintock arrived. She was on a mountaintop in the Pyrenees, having been sent there for her health and carried to the peak by porters. The news reached her in a terse telegram relayed by the British consul at Bayonne, who'd received an equally terse letter from M'Clintock. This gave her the details of his findings and added, almost as an afterthought, that her husband could not have suffered long and had died with success in sight.

She hurried back to London to find herself the most admired woman in the realm. She had triumphed where the Navy had failed. Persistently, year after year, she had pointed in the right direction, secure in the belief that her husband, a stickler for orders, would follow his instructions to the letter, even at the risk of his life.

He'd been told to go south, and south he'd gone. All along she had known he would. The relics of the expedition went on display at the United Services Institution, where the crowds were so thick it was necessary to issue tickets. The press was urging that Parliament reimburse her for the funds she had spent on the search. She replied she wouldn't accept a penny. But she did want to do something for M'Clintock and his crew. And she also wanted to do something more for her husband. She was determined that he, and not McClure, should be recognized as the man who first solved the puzzle of the Passage.

> *Whether Franklin had actually seen the last link of the Passage, before he died so mysteriously, was never argued. Obviously he hadn't.*

There were honours aplenty for the crew of the *Fox*. They were all granted the Arctic Medal. The officers were promoted. M'Clintock was toasted and honoured—with the freedom of the City of London, with honorary degrees from three leading universities in Britain, with a fellowship and a medal from the Royal Geographical Society, and a knighthood from the queen.

In March 1860, Lady Franklin, working behind the scenes as usual, prompted a debate in Parliament that resulted in an award of five thousand pounds to the crew of the *Fox*. Of that M'Clintock received fifteen hundred.

She herself was awarded the Patron's Medal of the Royal Geographical Society, becoming the first woman ever to receive that honour. With that went the prize she had sought for her husband—a memorial from the Royal Geographical Society, testifying to the fact that his expedition had indeed been the first to discover a North West Passage.

That made it clear there was no single channel to the Arctic, but several. Whether Franklin had actually seen the last link of the Passage, before he died so mysteriously, was never argued. Obviously he hadn't. He must have been aware, of course, that the channel in which his ships were trapped led inevitably to the Pacific along the coastline of North America. But to call him the discoverer of the Passage was stretching the known facts.

That downgraded McClure's later discovery of a passage farther north. Unlike Franklin, McClure had actually traversed the passage from west to east, though not entirely by water. But Franklin was a popular favourite. Indeed, the eleven-year search for the lost ships elevated him to Arctic sainthood.

To the *New York Times* he was "one of the ablest, oldest, and bravest men who had trodden that perilous path." The paper praised the expedition and the search that followed as being "as noble an epic as that which has immortalized the fall of Troy, or the conquest of Jerusalem."

The *Times* wrote of "unheard-of fortitude," "religious heroism," "courageous endeavour," and "devotion to duty," in the face of "appalling perils"—phrases of the day that were always brought out whenever another adventurer went to his death, planting his country's flag in the far corners of the world.

Cold they certainly were, even in their superior seal skins. But they were hardened to cold and knew how to prepare for it. The Inuit survived; the whites died to the last man. "They perished gloriously," to quote one of the letters to the Times.

And so for Franklin there would be a tablet at Greenwich, and a bust in Westminster Abbey, and a breathless fragment of poetry by Alfred Lord Tennyson, the poet laureate. No matter that the picture of the last days of the expedition, pieced together by M'Clintock, and later investigators, was bitterly ironic. For it is a picture of inadequately clothed, badly nourished men, dragging unmanageable loads down the bleak coast of an Arctic island.

As they stumble and drop in their tracks, other eyes watch them curiously. The Inuit of King William Island were also hungry, and there were times also when they too suffered from the scurvy and even froze to death. But they were never wiped out. Meagre though their diet had been that winter, it kept them alive and reduced the risks of disease.

Cold they certainly were, even in their superior seal skins. But they were hardened to cold and knew how to prepare for it. The Inuit survived; the whites died to the last man. "They perished gloriously," to quote one of the letters to the *Times*. That was the general attitude. But if they and their contemporaries had paid more attention to the Native way of life, they need not have perished at all.

INDEX

An engraving of Assistant Surgeon Elisha Kent Kane,
United States Navy (1829–1857). The engraving depicts Kane
during his 1850s missions to the Arctic in search of possible survivors
of the Franklin Expedition. Kane's hand rests on a monument, which
reads "Sacred to the memory of W. Braine R.N. H.M.S. Erebus ..."

DR. KANE OF THE ARCTIC SEAS

CONTENTS

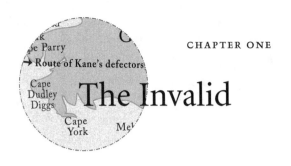

The Invalid

OF ALL THE NINETEENTH-CENTURY EXPLORERS WHO PROBED THE FROZEN WORLD OF THE CANADIAN ARCTIC, BY FAR THE BEST KNOWN WAS THE AILING, TWENTY-NINE-YEAR-OLD, AMERICAN SURGEON, ELISHA KENT KANE. HE LATER GAVE HIMSELF THE ROMANTIC TITLE OF "DR. KANE OF THE ARCTIC SEAS." ALTHOUGH HE IS ALL BUT FORGOTTEN NOW, THERE WAS A TIME WHEN HIS MEMOIRS WERE DEVOURED BY THOUSANDS OF ENTHUSIASTIC READERS.

Kane was his own best publicity agent. Both Roald Amundsen, the conqueror of the North West Passage, and Robert Peary, the polar explorer, were raised on Kane's version of his Arctic adventures. When he returned from his first trip to the Arctic in 1850, his dramatic descriptions of the harsh polar conditions electrified his generation. He was—and remained—a national hero, as much for his ability to tell a good story as for his explorations. By contrast, the British naval men who opened up the Arctic were far more restrained and tight-lipped. It was in their nature to make light of their troubles. As a result, Kane makes livelier reading.

On the face of it, this restless, driven man had no business being in the Arctic. He had a damaged heart and, indeed, would die before the decade was over. As a medical student suffering from rheumatic fever he'd gone to his bed each night never knowing whether he'd wake up the next morning. He was slender and fragile, though very handsome. He was a bit of a rebel who hated the discipline of the Navy. He grew seasick easily. In 1850, on his first expedition to the Arctic, he was so ill his commander tried to send him home. Kane stubbornly refused.

On the other hand, Kane was an adventurer. He had travelled to the ends of the earth—to Mexico, Egypt, the Mediterranean, Brazil, the African coast, the interiors of India and China. In ancient Egypt he had explored the catacombs of Thebes. He had stood at the entrance to the pass at

Thermopylae where a handful of Greeks held off a Persian army in the brave days of old. He had hiked across the storied peninsula known to the classical world as the Peloponnesus; and he had once hung suspended from a bamboo rope, attached to the two-hundred-foot (61-m) crag over a volcanic crater in the Philippines.

For much of that time he had been ill. He had contracted "tic fever" in Macao, "coast fever" in Africa, and "congestive typhus" during the Mexican War. In Mexico he was also wounded in the abdomen by a lance during hand-to-hand combat as the head of a guerrilla company.

Yet he kept on. One of his fellow students was convinced that his chronic heart problem led him to attempt reckless escapades. He would not put up with, he said, "the miserable tediousness of small adventures." Doomed to an early grave, he had nothing to lose. His journal suggests that he was out to prove something, not just to himself, but especially to his father, who had a low opinion of him.

In 1850 the Canadian Arctic was as mysterious as the moon. Two fur-trading explorers, Samuel Hearne and Alexander Mackenzie, had reached the northern tip of the continent in the previous century—but no one knew what lay beyond.

Some believed that the land might extend to the North Pole, for no one had actually explored the coastline. Some felt that another continent lay between North America and the Pole. Some believed in the myth of an "Open Polar Sea"—a warm Mediterranean lying beyond the ice pack. Some believed that the Arctic was wide open, without any land masses; others were convinced (rightly) that it was made up of islands.

For years every seaman had dreamed of a shortcut through North America to the fabled Orient, with its silks, spices, and treasures. They gradually realized that if there was such a North West Passage, it would be found somewhere beyond the Arctic mists.

Since the days of Elizabeth I, bold men in wooden ships had sought the elusive passage. But the real search did not begin until the world was at peace after Napoleon's overthrow in 1815. The Royal Navy, having little else to do, decided to map the unknown corners of the world. And so, ship after ship was sent north to explore the Canadian Arctic, and to find the elusive passage, if indeed such a passage did exist.

The British naval men were, by and large, a sensible lot. It must have been obvious to many that such a passage would not be practical. The land to the north was too cold and too remote.

Yet it drew them like a magnet. The idea of a lane of water leading directly to the riches of the East had been fixed in the folk memories of sailors for three centuries. Few could dismiss it from their imaginations.

Besides, whoever found the passage would become a hero, and a wealthy one at that. For the British honoured their heroes—especially their naval heroes—with practical rewards.

This helps to explain why John Franklin, a British naval captain in his sixtieth year, was eager to seek the passage. He was well past his prime and could easily have retired to a quiet existence in the country, but he couldn't resist the lure of the unknown.

He had already led two land expeditions to map the Canadian Arctic coast. But in 1845 he urged that he be given a chance to lead an expedition even farther north. The naval authorities humoured him, gave him two ships, the *Erebus* and the *Terror*, and sent him off, with great pomp and ceremony, to find the Passage.

Franklin and his 129 men vanished into the Arctic. None of them was ever seen alive again, nor was there any real hint at first of what had happened. He and his ships seem to have been swallowed up as surely as if they had been devoured by some carnivorous sea beast. It took search parties many years to piece together what likely happened to Franklin and his men.

The mystery of Franklin's fate aroused all of Europe into the most massive search in history. Eventually, other nations took part in a quest that occupied almost fifteen years.

Because no one knew where Franklin was, the frozen world was scoured from the western tip of Russian Alaska to its eastern entrance at Lancaster Sound. As a result, the Arctic was opened up, the islands mapped, the lanes of water charted, and Canada's boundaries stretched north to the Pole itself.

The Americans entered the search in 1850, five years after Franklin's disappearance. Henry Grinnell, a wealthy New York shipping magnate, egged on by Franklin's wife, Jane, bought two ships and sent them north to help the British. Elisha Kent Kane was eager to go along and signed on as chief medical officer.

Kane was as eager to go north as Franklin had been. These were years of high adventure and the Arctic held no terror for a man who had tempted a Philippine volcano. The Arctic itself had never known such activity. In 1850 when the Grinnell expedition headed north, no fewer than nine British ships were fitted out to take part in the search. Only one got back that year, while the other eight were imprisoned in the ice, their sledging parties fanning out in a fruitless hunt for the lost explorers.

Grinnell turned both his vessels, the *Advance* and the smaller *Rescue*, over to the United States government so that their crews might be placed under naval discipline. By August the expedition had reached Greenland and (while Kane fought seasickness) set off for Lancaster Sound in the heart of the Arctic. Most of the British ships were concentrated in that area and here the first clues to the Franklin puzzle were discovered.

Turning north up Wellington Channel, the searchers found what appeared to be a Royal Navy encampment on little Beechey Island. It was the first sign that Franklin had come this way. Kane was eager to inspect these early traces—circular mounds of limestone marking the position of tents, a crude fireplace, some bird bones, the rusting top of a food canister, and a few scraps of canvas.

Here they also came upon the graves of three of Franklin's men who had died in the first winter of his exploration. There could be no doubt that this was the site of Franklin's first winter camp.

Here they also came upon the graves of three of Franklin's men who had died in the first winter of his exploration. There could be no doubt that this was the site of Franklin's first winter camp. But where had he gone after that? No one really knew.

To avoid getting trapped by the freeze-up, all the ships were forced to move out to more open water. With masses of new ice groaning and grating her sides, the *Advance* struggled past ice tables fourteen feet (4.3 m) thick and hummocks that resembled cones of crushed sugar forty feet (12.2 m) high. Unlike the British, the Americans had no intention of wintering in the Arctic. It was time to return home.

Unfortunately, the smaller *Rescue* had become separated from her sister ship. She would have to be found before both were imprisoned by the ice.

"We're literally running for our lives," Kane wrote in his journal. "We're staggering along under all sail, forcing our way while we can." It was now so cold that coffee froze in the mugs.

At last the missing ship was found far to the west, sheltered by the cliffs of Griffith Island in Barrow Strait. The *Advance* took her in tow. Now the two little vessels headed eastward in a race against time and weather, leaving their British comrades behind.

Kane could hear the sounds of his own ship crunching through the new ice like a "rasping noise of close-grain sugar." His limbs grew stiff as he tried to warm them in his tiny cabin. And then the worst happened: the ice caught them. They were frozen in for the winter—"glued up," in Kane's phrase, at the mouth of Wellington Channel.

They were helpless—prisoners of the shifting ice pack. For the next two months the ice pushed them north into unexplored waters. Then it pushed them back again past their starting point. All around them, in their icy cradle, the roar of the surging pack rang in their ears, "a wild, yet not unmusical chorus," in Kane's description. It was almost as if the ice were alive, he thought, uttering animal-like shrieks or plaintive cries like those of a nighthawk.

The two little vessels were not equipped to ward off the stinging cold. As the winter advanced it grew fiercer. Food froze. No one had experienced cold as vicious as this, even in the chilly regions of the American Midwest. Barrels of fruit had to be chopped apart with an axe. Sauerkraut was as hard as rock. Butter and lard had to be carved with a cold chisel and mallet. When one seaman tried to bite into an icicle, a piece of it froze to his tongue. Two others lost all the skin on their lips. Facial hair turned to cardboard. If a man stuck out his tongue, it froze to his beard.

They feared to walk too far from the ship over the broken ice. Kane felt that the frost extended to his brain. A strange weariness fell over the crew whose members were infected by a desire to sit down and rest. Knowing that drowsiness and death could easily follow, they kept on their feet.

The men's features turned a ghastly white. Morale began to drop. It required an effort even to wash. At Christmas they put on a play and attempted a foot race. The effort exhausted them. One man actually fainted. Now the telltale signs of scurvy appeared—a swelling of the gums, soreness in the joints, fatigue. Simply climbing a ladder caused the strongest man to pant for breath.

"I long for the light," Kane wrote in his journal. "Dear, dear sun, no wonder you are worshipped!"

The crew of the *Rescue* was forced to abandon the ship, which had been badly battered by the ice. They crowded aboard the *Advance*—thirty-three men jammed into a room no bigger than Kane's father's library in Philadelphia. For them, there was no privacy.

On January 29, after eighty-six days of total darkness, the sun came back at last and the crew gave three hearty cheers. Kane did not take part. Instead he found a hummock of ice a mile (1.6 km) from the ship where he could drink in the rosy light of dawn by himself. "Never, till the grave-sod of the ice cover me, may I forego this blessing of blessings again!" he wrote dramatically.

"I long for the light," Kane wrote in his journal. "Dear, dear sun, no wonder you are worshipped!"

By February 10, the two ships—one crammed with thirty-three men, the other empty, drifting beside it—had been carried more than three hundred miles (480 km). Kane felt the scurvy in his limbs. It was as if he had taken a bad beating. Nineteen men now suffered from ulcerated gums. The worst were those who had eaten salt meat and hardtack without vegetables. Kane tried to treat this vitamin deficiency with olive oil and lime juice and those that took his advice began to get well.

March arrived. The *Advance* was still locked in the ice. A group of seamen went across to the *Rescue* and dug an eight-foot (2.4-m) pit around her hull so she might be repaired—a novel kind of dry dock. Then the first open leads of water appeared. In April the *Rescue*'s crew returned to their ship. On June 5 the breakup came so suddenly the men had to scramble to reload the ships.

Seated on the deck of the *Advance*, Kane saw a wondrous spectacle before him. A series of frozen waves seemed to be rippling across the white expanse. This astonishing spectacle—a seemingly solid surface swelling, rising, and falling, made him feel a bit seasick. Now the icebergs began to break up, shifting away to form a stream of moving ice.

The *Advance* was still attached to a submerged mattress of ice. The captain anchored a cable to an iceberg and let the swell of the water drive it against the ship like a great battering ram. Finally, after eight months and twenty-four days, they were free at last.

They had not found what they were searching for. Sir John Franklin and his crew were still missing. When they returned to New York on September 7, it was to report defeat.

CHAPTER TWO

The Spirit Rappers

ELISHA KENT KANE WAS DETERMINED TO RETURN NORTH. HE HAD BECOME OBSESSED BY THE IDEA OF ARCTIC EXPLORATION. HOWEVER, ANOTHER OBSESSION HAD ALSO CAPTURED HIM—ONE OF THE STRANGEST TO WHICH ANY ARCTIC EXPLORER HAD SUCCUMBED. HE HAD FALLEN HEAD OVER HEELS IN LOVE WITH AN EXTRAORDINARY NINETEEN-YEAR-OLD NAMED MARGARET FOX, WHO WAS AS FAMOUS IN HER OWN WAY AS THE ARCTIC HERO. SOME THOUGHT HER CLOSE TO BEING A SAINT. OTHERS SAW HER AS A MYSTIC. A FEW THOUGHT SHE WAS A SERVANT OF THE DEVIL. A FEW WERE CONVINCED SHE WAS A FRAUD.

For Margaret Fox was a medium, a "spirit rapper," who communicated, so it was said, with the souls of the dead. They rapped out messages from the spirit world using a simple code of numbers—one rap for "A", two for "B", and so on. Margaret and her younger sister Katherine were, indeed, the first of their kind—the model for all future mediums. For the cult of spiritualism began with the Fox sisters in 1848.

By the time Kane discovered the two sisters during their Philadelphia performance in November 1852, the craze had swept the nation. One million people believed in it. What started as a popular social fad had been transformed into a religious movement.

The nation was captivated by these innocent-looking young women, with their dark, lustrous eyes, their solemn features, and their remarkable clear skin, which gave them an otherworldly look. People tried to prove they were frauds but that only added to their appeal.

The two sisters sat at the séance tables with their hands and arms unconcealed, while the "spirits" spelled out the answers to questions thrown at them. Even when they were stripped of their clothing, as happened once, the rappings continued.

These "Rochester Rappings," as they were called, had begun at the Fox home near Rochester, New York, in 1848. The two girls—Katherine was then thirteen, Margaret sixteen—had scared their mother out of her wits when these mysterious sounds had appeared, apparently from nowhere. The girls had merely intended to tease their parents. But the results were so startling it got beyond control before they could reveal their secret. Nor did they confess it for another forty years.

The trick was very simple: the sisters both had double-jointed toes, which they learned to crack with little effort. And so, on this flimsy foundation, modern spiritualism was born—largely as the result of the exploitation of the two teenage girls by their older, widowed sister, Leah.

Kane did not believe in spirit rappings. He had dropped in on the sisters at the Union Hotel in Philadelphia out of sheer curiosity. When he saw Margaret reading by the window, she seemed so innocent that he thought he had knocked on the wrong door. It appears to have been a case of love at first sight.

> *The girls had merely intended to tease their parents. But the results were so startling it got beyond control before they could reveal their secret.*

His letters, later published after his death, suggest his passion: "I am sick … sick with hard work, and with nobody to nurse or care for me … is it any wonder that I long to look—only to look—at that dear little deceitful mouth of yours; to feel your hair tumbling over my cheeks …"

But there was the problem of the spirit rappings. Kane was convinced that Margaret was living a life of deception. Even as he planned his next assault on the Arctic, he tried to convince her to change her way of life.

"When I think of you dear darling, wasting your time and youth and conscience for a few paltry dollars and think of the crowds who come nightly to hear of the wild stories of the frozen north, I sometimes feel that we are not removed after all. My brain and your body are each the sources of attraction and I confess there is not so much difference," he wrote.

There were, of course, vast differences. She was an uneducated teenager, one of six children from the poverty-stricken family of an alcoholic. She didn't really know what she was doing and made no claims of any kind. He was an educated, well-travelled, and snobbish member of a prominent Philadelphia family. He longed to marry her. His family opposed it.

Throughout his life Kane had vainly sought his father's approval. Now his father wanted him to marry a wealthy Philadelphia girl. But Kane was in love with Margaret Fox. As far as Philadelphia society was concerned, she was the most unsuitable of all possible wives. It wasn't only that she was a notorious stage performer; there was also the matter of her upbringing.

So Kane decided he would change Margaret. He would go off to the Arctic, she would give up spirit rapping and, at his expense, enter a boarding school of his choosing far from the temptations of the big cities.

That did not sit well with Leah, the elder sister, who was making money from the séances. But Kane was firm: "Your life is worse than tedious, it is sinful, and that you have so long resisted its temptation shows me that you were born for better things than to entertain strangers at a dollar a head."

Meanwhile, during these winter months he was scribbling away on a book about his Arctic adventures and dashing from city to city delivering lectures. No wonder that in February and again in April he fell ill from the rheumatic fever that had weakened his heart.

Planning for the new Arctic expedition went on without him. Once again he would take the *Advance*—the ship from the previous expedition. But this would be a private venture; the U.S. Navy would only supply seamen. Fortunately, Henry Grinnell, the wealthy Arctic enthusiast who had provided funds for the first expedition, came up with more money.

In addition to the boats and sledges, pemmican and pickles, books and biscuits that were part of the expedition's supplies, Kane arranged for a more personal item. He paid an Italian painter to make a portrait of Margaret to take with him on the voyage, which was set for May.

With that done, he had her spirited away to a tiny village eighteen miles (29 km) from Philadelphia. There she was to receive an education from the wife of the local miller. That reduced her to tears, but Kane in one last letter attempted to comfort her:

"The day will come," he wrote "—bright as sunshine on the waters— when I claim your hand and unrestrained by the trammels of our mutual dread, live with you in peace, tranquillity and affection.

"Be good and pure. Restrain every thought which interferes with a guileless life, and live to prove your improvement, your love for—Ky."

CHAPTER THREE

The "Open Polar Sea"

AS HE PREPARED FOR HIS EXPEDITION, KANE KEPT INSISTING HIS MAIN PURPOSE WAS TO SEARCH FOR FRANKLIN.

He pretended to believe that Franklin and his lost crews were somewhere on the lost shores of the Open Polar Sea, living off its animal life, but unable to leave their hunting grounds and cross the frozen desert that was said to lie between the Open Polar Sea and the rest of the world.

Many of the explorers of that day were convinced, against all reason, that an "Open Polar Sea," as they called it, lay beyond the barrier of ice that blocked the way to the North Pole. According to this theory, a vast Arctic lake of still water lay somewhere beyond Smith Sound in the High Arctic. Here, so it was said, the air was milder and skies free of icy blasts. Kane saw this as a kind of Mediterranean. It was his intention to head for Smith Sound and try to break into the mysterious sea.

There was, of course, no Open Polar Sea. Like many of his colleagues, Kane was a victim of wishful thinking. It was pleasant to believe that somewhere, far to the north, the ice would vanish and the climate grow milder. But there wasn't a shred of evidence to support that belief—quite the opposite. Why would the ice suddenly melt as the Pole grew nearer? What would make the northern climate suddenly put on a southern face?

Kane's plan was to advance into the unknown by dogsled until he reached the mysterious sea. Then he would launch small boats and set out upon its waters. And so, on May 31, with a company of seventeen officers and men, and with crowds cheering and guns booming, he set off, declaring that "neither silence nor the vain glory of attaining an unreached North shall divert me from this one conscientious aim ..."

Was that his real purpose? One wonders. Kane knew that another explorer, a British naval officer, Commander Edward Inglefield, had already covered the territory he was heading for and found no clue of the missing Franklin expedition. It is likely that he was simply using the Franklin mystery as an excuse to raise funds for another discovery. While pretending to look for the lost expedition he gave every sign of seeking something even more difficult to reach—the North Pole itself.

When the *Advance* set sail from New York on May 31, 1853, Kane had not yet recovered entirely from his bout of rheumatic fever. He was also violently seasick as the little 144-ton (130.6-tonne) brig (a two-masted, square-rigged ship) tossed and rolled in the Atlantic. The slightest swell made him ill. Hardly anybody in the crew of seventeen thought he would recover. But recover he did.

It was not a very encouraging start for a man who had never before captained a ship, who knew little of navigation, and wasn't used to being a leader. He had little shipboard experience because in previous journeys as a doctor he had confined himself to the care of the sick. But now he found himself in command of a strange crew who had never worked together before. Many were amateurs and at least two were troublemakers.

One of these ruffians was a harbour boatman from the city's turbulent east side, named William Godfrey. The other was called John Hussey, but his real name was John Blake. Both of them would cause a great deal of trouble long before the expedition reached its goal.

On July 20, the ship reached Upernavik, the farthest north of the west Greenland settlements, well to the south of Melville Bay. Kane took on two new crew members—a plump and cheerful Inuit youth of nineteen, Hans Christian Hendrik, and Christian Petersen, a Danish dog driver who had considerable Arctic experience.

Petersen came reluctantly. He wasn't impressed by the expedition or by Kane or by his sailing master, John Wall Wilson, who knew nothing about ice. The crew was untrained—only the carpenter, Christian Ohlsen, had any real experience in polar navigation. And the food was inadequate; there were no fresh provisions—only salt meat.

Kane plunged ahead with all the enthusiasm of an amateur. In doing so he collided with a huge iceberg, losing a boat and jib boom. He blundered on through the middle ice of Baffin Bay until on August 6 he saw two huge fifteen-hundred-foot (457-m) capes—Alexander and Isabella—that formed the gateways to Smith Sound.

Godfrey and Blake were causing trouble. Godfrey was imprisoned for assaulting the sailing master, Wilson. But Kane couldn't keep him captive because he needed every man on deck.

He sailed through the great basin that today bears his name. By this time he had gone farther north than any other white man. But winter was closing in and the crew, exhausted from forcing the ship through the ice, was uneasy and homesick. They wanted to go back. Kane wanted to plunge forward.

In the end his officers persuaded him to stop. He couldn't go back because the ice was closing in, so he found a sheltered bay on the Greenland shore. He named it Rensselaer Harbour after his father's country estate. There he prepared to spend the gloomiest winter any of them had ever known.

Except for the people of Spitzbergen, north of Norway, warmed by a milder current, no white man had ever wintered this far north. They faced a gloomy winter. Even the pugnacious Godfrey was troubled by "blue devils." The unchanging polar landscape, he later wrote, was such that "the very soul of man seems to be suffocated by the oppressive gloom." Hans, the Inuit, was frightened to the point of weeping—homesick for his sweetheart. He tried to leave but Kane talked him out of it.

It was more than the polar darkness that cast a pall over the company. The men shivered in their quarters, eating cold food because Kane hadn't estimated the right amount of fuel for the journey. By the end of February they were out of oil, almost out of candles, and rapidly running out of coal. It wasn't possible to melt enough water in which to wash. They had to give up their tea. There was no more fresh bread. The galley stove was abandoned and all cooking done in the smoky main cabin.

Kane's own personality made things worse. The man who had portrayed himself in his memoirs as a selfless hero turned out to be snobbish, overbearing, boastful, and quite unable to keep his crew in order. Wilson thought him "peevish, coarse, sometimes insulting … the most self-conceited man I ever saw." By January the officers were eating their meals in silence to avoid a tongue-lashing from their captain.

By mid-winter several were suffering from scurvy. All but six of the fifty dogs had died from a mysterious illness. That meant the men themselves would have to manhaul the sledges when they struck north toward the fabled Open Polar Sea.

In February Kane began to prepare for the journey. This went against the advice of both Petersen and Ohlsen, who didn't like the idea of crossing the turbulent expanse of mountainous ice, jagged bergs, thick snowdrifts, and howling winds so early in the season. And there were other problems: Kane had to turn his cabin into a jail to hold the unruly Blake.

On March 19 he sent Henry Brooks, his first mate, and seven men to establish a shore depot for the polar dash. But Petersen was right—it *was* far too early. The weather was forty below Fahrenheit (-40° C). The snow was as sharp and as dry as sand. The terrain was unbelievably rough. The weather was so bad the men couldn't move their overloaded sledge. And so they turned back, four of the party so frostbitten they couldn't walk.

Petersen, Ohlsen, and a young German scientist, August Sonntag, left the others behind and pushed on for help. The ship was thirty miles (48 km) away. If their friends were to survive they wouldn't have time to stop for food, drink, or sleep. They made the trip in thirteen hours, arriving delirious and haggard. Ohlsen had to have his toes amputated because of frostbite. The other two were unable to speak.

Kane gathered up seven seamen and set off with the crippled Ohlsen lashed to the sledge. In spite of his amputated toes the carpenter would have to serve as guide because the others were powerless. The sledge was useless in the tangle of broken ice. The party abandoned it and struggled forward on foot. Ohlsen, half fainting, was supported between two men.

At last they found the tent containing the missing men, half expecting the occupants to be dead. They were grateful to discover them just barely alive. After sleeping in two-hour shifts, they strapped the invalids to their sledge and the party set off for the ship.

This was a nightmare journey. Again and again they were forced to unload the sledge and lift it over a barrier, while the sick lay groaning on the ice. After ten miles (16 km) even the healthy men began dropping in their tracks. Kane and Godfrey raised a tent to cover them up. Then Kane headed out for another nine miles (14.4 km) to pick up the abandoned sledge which they had left behind on the outward journey. Godfrey offered to go with him. Although he was a problem, Kane accepted because he was tougher than the others.

Before they reached their goal, Kane was delirious—babbling and swooning. But Godfrey pushed him along. At one point, Kane thought Godfrey was a bear and called on his imaginary crew to shoot him. By this time his beard was so solidly frozen to his clothing that when they reached the missing sledge Godfrey had to hack off part of it with a jackknife.

Finally the others caught up. They moved forward at the rate of about a mile and a half (2.4 km) an hour, all demented, seized by a kind of frenzy, laughing frantically, groaning and screaming—a company of madmen.

The safety of the ship was in the hands of the young ship's doctor, Isaac Hayes. He was only twenty-one—a green medical student just out of school. When the half-crazed men reached the ship they looked like corpses, covered from head to foot with frost, their beards lumpy with ice, their eyes vacant and wild. They threw themselves on their bunks and passed out.

To Hayes, the ship "presented all the appearances of a mad house." Two men died, but Kane, the long-time invalid, was the last to collapse and the first to recover.

Shortly after this, a seaman spotted eight people on the shore—Inuit from the community of Etah seventy miles (112 km) away, the most northerly permanent human habitation in the world. They had never before seen white men. They cheerfully sold Kane four dogs to add to the three healthy animals left on the ship.

When Kane recovered he planned another expedition. Far to the north lay the great Humboldt Glacier—the most massive ice sheet in the known world. Kane was anxious to visit it. On April 25, he sent a party of six ahead with some of the dogs and followed on after with Godfrey as his sole companion. Even though Godfrey was a problem he had saved Kane's life and was the fittest man and the best dog driver on the ship.

The scenery was spectacular. Red sandstone cliffs, cut by bays and fissures, rose a thousand feet (305 m) from the frozen sea. Ahead, the great glacier sprawled across Greenland, its glittering face looking down on them from a height of four hundred feet (122 m). But they couldn't climb it.

Three men had gone blind, another suffered chest pains, several were crippled by scurvy. On May 4, Kane himself almost fainted and, with one foot frozen, was strapped into the sledge. When he reached the ship ten days later he was in a stupor.

He had failed again. With two of his crew dead and most of the rest shattered, he only had three men healthy enough for duty. Four of the officers were "knocked up," in his phrase. Almost a year had gone by and he had little to show for it. He hadn't found Franklin and, indeed, he hadn't made much effort to find him. He'd seen no evidence of the Open Polar Sea.

Could Franklin have survived? he asked himself. It occurred to him the Inuit might be caring for the lost expedition. He knew that the hundred-mile (160-km) blank spot on his crude map of the Kane Basin must be filled in if he was to salvage anything from his ill-fated adventure. He sent William Morton, his steward, and Hans Hendrik, the Greenland Native, to sledge north to the very top of the basin. This time he knew they *must* succeed.

They staggered back on July 10, their dogs limping, one animal in such bad shape he had to be carried. But they had sensational news. They had found a new channel thirty miles (48 km) wide leading north out of the basin. They had followed it until they had reached a massive cliff—Cape Constitution—jutting into the water. At that point they had gone eighty miles (128 km) farther north than any other white explorer.

Morton, clawing his way for five hundred feet (152 m) up the rocky precipice, had seen a marvellous spectacle—open water as far as the eye could view. The cliffs were a-flutter with sea fowl; the glittering sea was free of ice. Kane was certain that what Morton had seen was the Open Polar Sea.

Of course he was wrong. The magical waters Morton saw in the distance were simply the product of wind, waves, and wishful thinking.

Such mirages are common in the Arctic, as they are in the desert, and for similar reasons. They are caused when the air close to the ground is denser than the air above. Sailors often saw distant ships upside down, as in a spyglass, and apparently floating in the sky—or even ranges of non-existent mountains on the horizon.

Kane, however, believed Morton's discovery more than justified the horrors he had been through. "I can say that I have led an expedition whose results will be remembered for all time," he wrote.

Food and fuel were growing scarce and it was obvious that the officers and crew were unreliable. Kane knew he must try again to justify the expedition—especially to his family who viewed it with such foreboding. "I hope, if I have the health to fill up my notes that I may advance myself in my father's eyes by a book on glaciers and glacial geology," he wrote. But he was faced with the dreadful possibility of a second winter in the Arctic.

By August, except for a little hot coffee and soup, the men were existing on cold salt pork. Then they found they could not blast their ship out of the frozen ice of the harbour. Kane realized the worst: "It is *horrible*—yes, that is the word—to look forward to another year of disease and darkness to be met without fresh food and without fuel."

Was he also to suffer the fate of Franklin? The winter was closing in. He left an account of his discoveries in a cairn, encased in glass and sealed up with melted lead. On the nearby cliff in huge letters he painted the name of his ship. The coffins of the two dead crew members lay buried beneath. How many more graves would there be before the winter was over?

CHAPTER FOUR

"The Most Perfect Hellhole"

KANE'S DEALINGS WITH HIS CREW—ESPECIALLY THE OFFICERS—GREW WORSE. THE MEN WERE INSOLENT, REFUSING TO ATTEND EVENING PRAYERS. IN FACT, THE CREW DESPISED THEIR CAPTAIN. JOHN WILSON, KANE'S SAILING MASTER, CLAIMED THAT KANE COULDN'T WALK THROUGH THE SHIP "WITHOUT HEARING HIS NAME USED IN THE MOST INSOLENT MANNER BY THE MEN IN THE FORECAS-TLE." AS FOR THE OFFICERS, HE WROTE, "THERE WASN'T ONE WHO WOULD TRUST ONE WORD HE SAID OR PLACE A PARTICLE OF CONFIDENCE IN HIM. HE DOES NOTHING BUT QUARREL FROM MORNING TO NIGHT WITH THOSE AROUND HIM." WHEN THE CAPTAIN WASN'T QUARRELLING HE WAS BOASTING—ABOUT HIS NARROW ESCAPES, HIS GLOBAL ADVENTURES, HIS RECEPTION BY FOREIGN HEADS OF STATE, AND THE COSTLY DINNERS AT WHICH HE HAD BEEN THE HOST.

We must remember that discontent of this kind was common among seamen cooped up for twelve months or more on a tiny, uncomfortable wooden ship in a strange and hostile land. The history of Arctic exploration is full of such problems. But there is no doubt that Kane was a difficult captain and one who had little experience in handling men.

The constant arguments were too much for Christian Ohlsen, the carpenter who Kane had appointed to replace Henry Brooks as first mate. Ohlsen quit that job in June. Kane soon became aware of secret meetings in Ohlsen's quarters and also in Isaac Hayes's. Men would gather in groups whispering together. Finally, Morton came to report that several wanted to leave the ship rather than spend another winter in the Arctic. Their plan was to make their way to Upernavik, the northernmost of the Greenland settlements, seven hundred miles (1,120 km) to the south.

To Kane these men were traitors. Yet he knew that if he refused them permission to leave, there would be even worse problems. On August 24, he

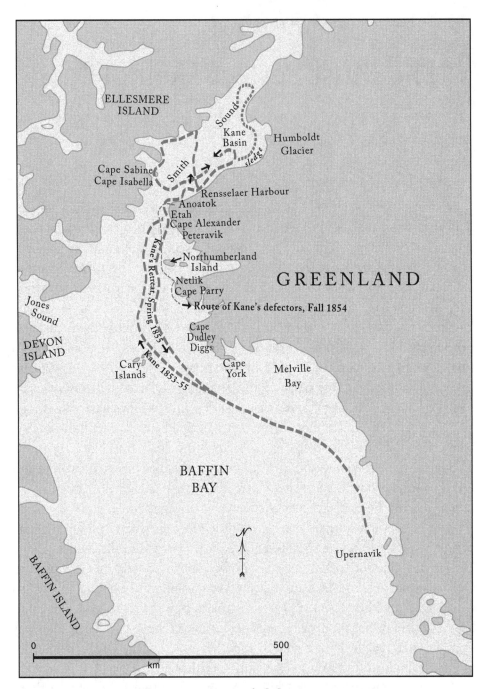

The Arctic Voyages of Elisha Kent Kane

called his company together to warn them of the dangers they faced and gave them twenty-four hours to make up their minds.

He got his answer the following day. All but five men agreed to leave. Of the loyalists, only Morton and "Irish Tom" Hickey, the cabin boy, were fit for duty. The others were too ill to work.

To Kane's dismay, four of his officers were determined to leave. He could understand Hayes: he was a doctor and the party would need him. But he felt the other officers' decisions were close to treachery. Finally two men, Wilson and James McGary, agreed to stay.

Now nine of the ship's company were preparing to leave. Kane wouldn't even talk to them. He agreed to give them some food and equipment and a boat, which Ohlsen would build. He advised them to elect a leader and they chose Ohlsen.

Ohlsen couldn't make up his mind. Kane now insisted that he and the others sign a statement that from the moment they left the ship they would be under their own control and their connection with the expedition would be regarded as closed. When Ohlsen refused, Kane withdrew his permission for Ohlsen to leave, warning that he would shoot him as a deserter. Ohlsen had no choice but to remain.

The others took three days to get organized. The goodbyes were remarkably friendly. Kane even broke out his private stock of champagne. Inwardly he seethed with a black rage. He saw them as deserters who had betrayed him by leaving their posts and he washed his hands of them.

The captain saw himself as a martyr victimized by traitors. "I have made up my mind to act towards these miserable men without a thought of self … God will take care of us. I did not know before this awful prospect of a second winter that I had so much faith," he wrote.

The departing crew members quarrelled among themselves. Actually, they became panic-stricken when their small sledge went through the ice and almost drowned them. One man, George Riley, went back to the ship. But the seven remaining deserters vanished into the mists of the south. On September 5, 1854, all connections were cut.

Kane was outwardly calm. But into his journal he poured out all his feelings of betrayal, his sense of personal injury, and his self-justification of the events of the previous weeks.

"… They are deserters, in act and in spirit—in all but the title. They leave their ship, abandon their sick comrades, fail to adhere to their commander, and are false to the implied trust which tells every true man to abide by the Expedition into which he has entered … this misguided party have wanted for nothing—they have had the best of everything, even at self sacrifice … They should have had the same treatment had they spit in my face."

He was certain they would come back, many of them broken down, to seek a refuge on board. He would give it to them but he would never trust them again. In his mind they were "low minded sneaks."

Now Kane had to protect the ship for the winter. He turned part of it into a reasonable copy of an Inuit igloo. The crew tore the planking off the upper deck to use as firewood. They sealed the quarterdeck with a padding of moss and turf. Then they built a living space just eighteen feet (5.5 m) square, lining the ceiling and floors with moss and caulking the floor with oakum and plaster of Paris. To reach these cramped quarters the crew would have to crawl through a long, narrow passage between the decks. This would be their home for the next eight or ten months.

Kane also knew he would have to depend on the Inuit for fresh seal and walrus meat to stave off scurvy, and also for dogs to haul sledges. But he discovered, to his dismay, that a band of Natives with whom he had been dealing had made off with his cooking utensils and buffalo robes. He knew he'd have to stop any further pilfering.

He sent his two best hikers, Morton and Riley, to the tiny community of Anoatok, halfway between the ship and the main Inuit village of Etah. There they found three of the culprits—a boy and two women asleep with their loot.

They took drastic steps. They sent the boy to Etah to report to the headman, Metek, and then kidnapped the two women. One of these was Metek's wife. She would be used as bait to bring the headman back to the brig with a sledload of the stolen goods.

With that done, Kane made a formal treaty with the Inuit. They promised to supply him with fresh meat and dogs and to stop stealing. On his part he swore to give them presents and guns with which to hunt.

There was a worse problem. A body of rats had left the ship's hold for the warmth of Kane's makeshift igloo. There were rats everywhere—under the stove, in the cushions, in the lockers, in the bedding. They chewed away at furs, woollens, shoes, specimens—everything. When Kane put his hand into his mitten one day he was bitten by a mother rat that was raising her brood inside. And before he could stop the blood the rat family ran off with the mitten!

Kane put the rats to good use. After all, he'd been all over the world eating everything from bats to puppy dogs. He had already become used to eating raw blubber with the Inuit, and so now he simply cooked and ate the rats. Many of the company suffered from scurvy but Kane didn't, thanks to the fresh meat.

As the weeks dragged by, the ship was slowly stripped of all firewood. The upper deck, bulwark, fancy shelving, and bulkheads were gone by early November. The crew's morale was shattered. One man, McGary, became so homesick he refused to eat anything.

Kane confessed to moments of despair: "My thoughts, my diseased craving for love and caressment, everything that unbends, I crush, strangle, before they take shape. The Father—I cease to remember his years—the Mother—I will not count her tears—weeping on her wet pillow for her first-born and her last."

He had already become used to eating raw blubber with the Inuit, and so now he simply cooked and ate the rats. Many of the company suffered from scurvy but Kane didn't, thanks to the fresh meat.

But as captain he couldn't allow these feelings to show. In fact he continued his dictatorial style, which added to the tensions. Kane took out his inner rage on the youngest member of the crew, Tom Hickey. But nobody really escaped his outbursts.

To Wilson, the cramped cabin was "the most perfect hellhole." About Kane, he wrote: "From the time he gets up in the morning till we are all turned in he is incessantly quarrelling with someone or making use of his arbitrary power." Kane never went to bed until three or four in the morning and never rose until after noon. And that caused problems, for he made everybody else get up early.

He saw himself through different eyes, as a stern parent keeping his difficult children in line. "… If the Lord does not blot me out and I will return as a man who has braved a hard temptation and abided by his trust, then those who live either with me, or after me … will give me credit for something more than a blind will & a groping materialism …"

Kane was lonely. He was cut off from the one man with whom he might have been friends. This was Henry Goodfellow, whom Kane had taken on as a natural history observer as a favour to Kane's brother, Tom. Goodfellow was worse than useless. Wilson found him "lazy, dirty, ragged and impudent to everyone." Kane thought him "one of the most impractical and helpless men I was ever connected with."

As the days went by, Goodfellow neglected his duty, refused to look after himself, and withdrew from his shipmates, most of whom wouldn't speak to him. Finally Kane took over Goodfellow's duties himself and while the others toiled, Goodfellow lounged about, reading novels.

Though Kane could never speak to him "without disgust," he still catered to him. He had looked upon Goodfellow as his closest friend, a man of his own social class. Now he was doing his jobs for him, even carrying glasses of lime juice and water when asked. "He has more cool impudence than any man I ever knew," Kane wrote of his former friend.

By early December, five of the crew were sick with scurvy. The only medicine available was the gratings from raw potatoes. Scurvy comes about from a lack of fresh vegetables and fruits. There were only old potatoes left and these were three years old at least. But that was all they had.

The three healthy men were put to work tearing the oak ribbing off the ship for firewood. Kane managed to collect a ton (907 kg) of fuel this way. He knew it wouldn't last past January. For February and March he counted on using three inches (7.6 cm) of oak sheathing nailed to the ship's side as protection against ice. That would give them two and a half more tons (2.3 tonnes) of firewood.

At three o'clock in the morning of December 7, Kane was awakened with the news that five sledges with six teams of dogs, each with strange drivers, were approaching the ship. A few minutes later, a group of Inuit came aboard supporting his former shipmates, Bonsall and Petersen, both of whom were in dreadful condition. They had left the brig fourteen weeks before, but as Kane had prophesied they hadn't been able to get to

Upernavik. They reported that the others, exhausted and starving, were crouched in a stone hovel some hundred and fifty miles (240 km) to the south. The pair had managed to get back to the brig by bribing the southern Inuit. Now they pleaded for help for their comrades.

Kane acted at once, gathered up a hundred pounds (45 kg) of provisions, and sent them off with the Natives. Petersen and Bonsall were so sick they couldn't move. Kane and the able-bodied men couldn't desert the sick aboard the ship. He didn't really trust the new Natives to take the food back to the others, but he had no choice. He gave them presents, sent them on their way, and hoped for the best.

CHAPTER FIVE

Saved by the Inuit

What had happened to the "deserters" who had left for the south the previous August? The eight men were an odd lot—a German astronomer, a Baltimore seaman, a Pennsylvania farmer, a Greenland cooper, a Hull sailor, an East River boatman, an Irish patriot, and a Philadelphia medical student.

Only the Greenlander, Petersen, had any Arctic experience, but he was not the one who was really in charge. The man on whom they depended for life or death was a cheerful and talkative Inuit medicine man from the village of Netlik. His name was Kalutunah. Kane and his crew met him the first winter. Now the deserters ran into him again as they struggled slowly in their two small boats through the tangled wilderness of ice. By the time they reached Netlik on the coast near Northumberland Island, they were running short of food and fuel. Kalutunah's people gave them blubber to eat and moss for lamp wicks in return for needles and knives.

Four days later, on September 16, the ice closed in for good. Now they knew they had no hope of getting to civilization before spring. They went to work in the bitter cold, trying to build a shelter on the shore using huge stones chinked with moss, and some tin and lumber taken from the two boats.

Finally, on October 9, they moved into what Dr. Hayes called, "a cold, fireless, damp, vault-like den." By October 18 they had eaten all their biscuits and now had to survive on rock moss which produced dreadful stomach cramps. Certain death faced them.

Then, two days later, they were saved when two strangers covered from head to foot in a coating of ice and snow, crawled into the hut. This was Kalutunah and a companion. They'd travelled for thirty-six hours without stopping to bring frozen meat and blubber. The men fell on it like wolves.

Clearly they couldn't survive without help from the Natives, who were eager for white men's goods. Petersen was the only one who spoke their language. He arranged a treaty in which the white men would be supplied with food in exchange for knives, needles, and other treasures. But Kalutunah wouldn't rent them any dogs or sledges. Obviously, he didn't want them to get away.

After supplying the party with enough meat for one meal and some blubber for fuel, the two Inuit left. It was two weeks before they returned. In the meantime the men, who didn't know enough to hunt, survived on rock moss, growing steadily weaker. They recovered when the Inuit came back with several days' supply of blubber.

It was maddening. The Inuit gave them only enough food or fuel to keep them alive. Here they were—eight men from the civilized world—trapped in a tiny shack, unable to bring in more than an occasional fox or ptarmigan in spite of their superior weapons.

They knew they had to get away. Their only chance was to send back to the ship for more supplies, and try to reach the whaling fleet in the spring.

Yet the Inuit came and went at will, apparently unaffected by the weather. One day a young woman turned up with a six-month-old baby strapped to her back. She had travelled forty miles (64 km)—in thirty-five-below-Fahrenheit (–37° C) weather—often getting off the dogsled and walking. The only reason for her trip was to see the white strangers.

They knew they had to get away. Their only chance was to send back to the ship for more supplies, and try to reach the whaling fleet in the spring. Petersen agreed to go to the village with Kalutunah and bargain for dogs and sleds. Godfrey offered to go with him.

The two men reached the village on November 3. At first they were well fed and well treated. But as time passed, Petersen, a cautious Dane who had lived among the Inuit for twenty years and was married to one, began to feel uneasy. Many strangers began to crowd into the village including a glowering dog driver named Sip-su, who boasted that he'd killed two members of his own tribe because they couldn't hunt. And Kalutunah seemed to be under Sip-su's spell.

Petersen was anxious to be on his way, but now nobody volunteered to go with him. He quietly warned Godfrey in the next hut to be on his guard and told the Natives that if anything happened to him his friends would arrive with their magic guns and kill them all.

His only security lay in the Inuit's belief that he had a pistol. The Natives were convinced it was a magic wand, for they had never seen a gun. It was this fear that saved him. Actually he had no pistol, and the rifle, which the Natives feared, lay outside the hut.

Pretending to sleep, Petersen heard Sip-su telling the others that he would lead an attack on the white men with Kalutunah as his lieutenant. Petersen opened his eyes just as Sip-su started to search his clothing for the non-existent pistol. Outside the hut a crowd had gathered around Petersen's rifle, afraid to touch it. Petersen seized it and announced he was going off to hunt for bear.

He alerted Godfrey and the two set off immediately on a forty-mile (64-km) trek back to Hayes and the others. They had gone no more than two miles (3.2 km) before the Natives gave chase. Petersen brandished the magic rifle and that kept them at a distance.

But the pair could not sleep. If the Natives didn't get them, the cold would. Drowsy, exhausted, starving, and mad with thirst, they reached their goal after trudging for twenty-four hours. "Water! Water!" they cried as they stumbled into the hut. They had survived only because they had been fed well during the previous three days.

The party of seamen prepared for an attack. Instead, Kalutunah appeared, all smiles, and brought them a large piece of walrus meat. Hayes was convinced that the Inuit had been influenced by a bad leader and he was right. It turned out that Kalutunah had opposed Sip-su's ideas. Fortunately for everybody, Sip-su's courage had failed him in the presence of the magic gun.

Now the party managed to get five dogs from the Natives. But it was not possible to get back to the brig. After a few miles the attempt failed, and they returned, stupefied by cold. The following morning the two strongest men, Petersen and Bonsall, set off by themselves for Kane's ship. Those left behind again had no food except for pieces of walrus hide, and by the third day even that was gone.

The desperate men believed now that the Inuit intended to leave them to their fate. The Natives wouldn't take the party north, or rent them dog teams. It seemed they were determined to let the men starve to death before plundering the hut. But Hayes had no intention of allowing that. He didn't want to murder the Inuit. But his plan was to put them to sleep with laudanum, a form of opium. Then they would steal the Inuit dogs and sleds and head for the ship.

He made a soup of the two pieces of meat that the Inuit allowed them. He slipped the contents of a vial of the laudanum into their soup bowls. Then while the whites watched, the Natives ate greedily and soon became drowsy. Hayes and the others helped them off with their coats and boots and then moved quickly to put on their own travelling clothes.

They knew they had no time to lose. They crawled out of the hut, taking the Natives' boots, mittens, and coats with them. Then they barricaded the doorway as best they could.

The journey that followed was clumsy. No one understood how to handle Inuit dogs. One sledge overturned and the dogs squirmed out of their traces and fled back to the hut. With three men on each of the remaining two sledges the party blundered on as far as Cape Parry where they found shelter in a cave.

Their freedom was short-lived. The Inuit had awoken quickly and, with their usual ingenuity, made mukluks out of blankets, cut up other blankets as ponchos, found the lost sled and the wandering dogs, and quickly picked up the party's trail.

Since they knew how to handle the dogs, it was no trick to catch up with the white men. There they stood, silent accusers, their heads sticking out of the blankets—one red, one white, one blue—their feet wrapped in old cloths and, in one case, a discarded pair of boots, and their arms filled with the treasure they could not bear to abandon—tin cups, saucers, cutlery, even an old hat. The situation would have been ludicrous had it not been so threatening.

Hayes held them off with a rifle. The Inuit pleaded with them not to shoot. Hayes took two prisoners, and in sign language offered a deal. If Kalutunah would drive the party north, they would return the dogs, sledges, and clothes. Otherwise, they would shoot them all. Kalutunah cheerfully agreed.

Now they moved north through a series of small Inuit settlements. The Inuit there treated them well. Finally, they reached the larger village of Etah, but not without a terrifying journey around Cape Alexander, where they were forced to cling to a narrow shelf on the cliffside, no more than fifteen inches (38 cm) wide, high above the sea.

When they reached Etah they discovered that Petersen's Inuit had eaten all the food that Kane had sent back. They still had seventy miles (112 km) to go! By the time they reached the brig one man was stupefied by cold, the others were at a breaking point.

"We come here destitute and exhausted to claim your hospitality," Hayes said. "We know we have no rights to your indulgence, but we feel that with you we will have a welcome and a home."

Kane took one look at him—covered with snow, fainting from hunger—grasped his hand and beckoned his companions aboard. The young doctor's feet were so badly frostbitten that Kane had to amputate several of his toes. He gave Hayes his own bed to sleep in.

But he did not forgive him.

CHAPTER SIX

Retreat

HALF AN HOUR PASSED. THEN THE SINGLE MAST OF A SMALL SHALLOP SHOWED ITSELF. PETERSEN BEGAN TO SOB AND TO CRY OUT, HALF IN ENGLISH, HALF IN DANISH. KANE FORGAVE NO ONE. HE NOW HAD EIGHT MORE MEN ON HIS CROWDED SHIP THAN HE HAD PLANNED FOR. THEY HAD NO FOOD OR EQUIPMENT, AND ONLY THE CLOTHES ON THEIR BACKS—NOT EVEN BLANKETS. THEY HAD LOST EVERYTHING THEY HAD TAKEN WITH THEM. HE HAD EXPECTED TO LAST OUT THE WINTER WITH A SMALL, BUT FAITHFUL, COMPANY AND THEN MAKE A DASH FOR THE SEA. NOW HE HAD ALMOST DOUBLE THE NUMBER HE HAD RECKONED ON.

The loyal party that had stayed with Kane was bitter at the returnees.

"God in Heaven," the explorer wrote in his private journal, "it makes my blood boil!" He took out his anger with his pencil, in page after page, railing against the men who had defected. "These men can never be my associates again," he wrote.

And so, in that cramped little vessel with its one crowded room, he ordered a strange arrangement. He would divide the ship's company into two groups—the faithful and the unfaithful. Each would eat separately. The unfaithful wouldn't be allowed to do any work on the ship. They could contribute to their own routine, but would be treated merely as guests. The faithful would do all the work, but since most were down with scurvy, or useless, that meant that Kane himself must take on most of the burden.

There was another problem. The two malcontents, Blake and Godfrey, were so unpopular they had to eat by themselves. That caused a battle in which Kane bashed in Blake's skull with a belaying pin and knocked Godfrey to the ground. Blake suffered a concussion but recovered. Kane told him if he disobeyed again he would kill him.

As the winter wore on, tempers continued to fray. Wilson was convinced

Kane's brain had become unhinged. Fresh meat was scarce. Even Hans, the Inuit hunter, couldn't find much. And at Etah, the Inuit too were starving.

Although the crew still remained divided between the faithful and the unfaithful, to use Kane's terms, he had to call upon the healthier of the former deserters to help with the work. By March, fourteen men were flat on their backs with scurvy.

He faced a more serious problem. Godfrey and Blake were planning to steal dogs, a sledge, and provisions, and leave for the south.

Kane rose on the morning of March 20, armed himself, and ordered Godfrey to cook breakfast. Then he crawled through the narrow passageway between decks that led to the sleeping quarters and waited. Blake appeared first and then Godfrey. Kane leaped out and thrust a pistol an inch from Godfrey's nose. When Godfrey confessed to a plot, Kane knocked him down and hammered him with a piece of lead concealed inside his mitt. But he faced a real problem. He couldn't jail either man because he needed them to help. As a result, Godfrey managed to slip away. When Kane sent Hans south with sledges to get meat at Etah, Godfrey caught up with him and took his team.

Kane threatened to shoot him but his rifle wouldn't fire in the cold. Godfrey walked away just as a bullet whistled over his head. He made it back to Etah.

Hans didn't come back. Only a few ptarmigan shot by Petersen kept the invalids alive. Then, on April 2, a man was seen a mile from the brig. Was it Hans? No—it was William Godfrey with two dogs and a sled-load of walrus meat. He had made a seventy mile (112 km) trip on foot in fifty-degree-below-Fahrenheit (–46°C) weather to reach Etah in just thirty hours—something no one else had been able to do. He reported that Hans was ill and that he, himself, had decided to live with the Inuit. Kane threatened to shoot him but his rifle wouldn't fire in the cold. Godfrey walked away just as a bullet whistled over his head. He made it back to Etah.

The meat that he'd brought was a godsend. Kane was suspicious of both the absent Godfrey and his crony, Blake, who was still aboard ship. He was convinced they were planning some mischief. He needed to put up a show of discipline; otherwise others might follow Godfrey's example. He called his men together and warned that anyone who deserted would be shot.

He couldn't let Godfrey get away with it, and so on April 10 set off for Etah by himself. There he found Hans hunting seal. He wasn't ill any more, but he was in love with a young Inuit woman named Merkut who had nursed him when he was sick. Kane got Hans back to the brig and then again turned his attention to Godfrey.

Kane now disguised himself as an Inuit, took one of Hans's friends with him, armed himself with a six-shooter, packed a set of leg irons, found Godfrey in a hut at Etah, and forced him back at gunpoint.

Hans would not stay on the ship. He set off to Etah, apparently to get some walrus hide to make some boots. Actually, he wanted to return to Merkut, and this was the last Kane saw of him. The two were married and went off to raise a family, and that was that.

Now Kane knew that he would have to abandon the ship. She was a sorry-looking sight that May—her upper spars, bulwarks, deck sheathing, stanchions, bulkheads, hatches, ice timbers, and railings had all been torn away for fuel. Every bit of rope, everything burnable down to the last broomstick, had been sacrificed to keep the crew from freezing to death.

They would have to make their way south to Upernavik by small boat.

Kane got the healthier men building runners to haul two large boats and a smaller dinghy over the snows to reach open water. That lay eighty miles (128 km) to the south at Naviliak, on the coast not far from Etah.

They faced a terrible ordeal: everything—three boats, fifteen hundred pounds (680 kg) of supplies, and four invalids—would have to be shuttled a mile or so between rests, by men already weakened by scurvy and hunger. The sick were placed in a halfway house in Anoatok. It took the others thirty-one days to move everything to the open sea. In that time—May 17 to June 18—the exhausted men, so weak they could only pull one boat at a time, each trudged a distance of 316 miles (509 km).

Kane did more than that. He travelled constantly by dogsled—to Etah to get food, to Anoatok to look after the invalids, then back to the brig to help bake bread. Altogether this remarkable man covered 1,100 miles (1,770 km). Then, on the final lap, Christian Ohlsen came to grief. One of the runners of his boat had broken through the surface and only his strength kept it from swamping, while the others pulled it back to solid ice. But Ohlsen had ruptured his bladder and a few days later he died.

Kane later acknowledged that without the Inuit they would never have made it. The entire population of Etah turned out to wave them goodbye as the two whaleboats, *Faith* and *Hope*, set off on June 19. For the next forty-nine days they fought their way through blizzards, pack ice, and bergs.

Kane insisted that every man get his rest at night, even though it meant lying under ice-sheathed cliffs in their buffalo robes, or sleeping aboard the boats. To keep up the crew's morale, the captain continued morning and evening prayers. No longer idle, the company knew now their only hope of survival lay in working as a team.

Soon their food was almost exhausted. Kane allowed each of his crew only six ounces (170 g) of bread dust a day, plus a walnut-sized lump of tallow. The men were losing their muscular power as they dragged their boats through veins of water between the ice fields. Kane knew they would have to find food quickly or die.

The flotilla tied up to a great ice floe, from whose peak he could see in the distance the red face of Cape Dalrymple Rock. At that very point a gale hit the flotilla. The ice floe was hurled and crushed against the base of the rock and the men were helplessly whirled about in their boats. Using boat hooks they forced themselves into a stretch of open water. When the tide rose they pulled their craft over an ice shelf and into a gorge where, too weak to unload their supplies, they dropped in their tracks and slept.

Fortunately there was food. They gathered ducks' eggs—twelve hundred in a single day—and shot sea fowl. To keep them going on the next leg of their voyage they now had two hundred pounds (90 kg) of dried meat.

At Cape Dudley Diggs, the tongue of a great glacier barred their way. Kane, climbing a berg, saw to his dismay that here the season was late. The ice still blocked their way; they would have to wait for the delayed summer to open a lane. He could not bear to tell the others. They waited another week, crept forward in their battered craft to Cape York, and waited again.

It was July 21. There was game but no fuel. To cook the meat, they were forced to burn oars, sledge runners, and finally the little dinghy, *Red Eric*. They set off again and found, after an exhausting journey, that they had mistakenly entered a false inlet that led nowhere. The prospect of repairing the sledges and retracing their steps with the boats again on runners was so horrifying that even McGary, the toughest of the crew, was reduced to tears.

It took three days of backbreaking toil.

By the time they crossed Melville Bay their food was gone. Only the lucky capture of a seal saved them from starving to death. Then at last, on August 1, they sighted the famous landmark known as the Devil's Thumb, a huge bulbous peak that told them they'd entered the whaling grounds of Baffin Bay.

Two days later, Petersen came upon the first Native they'd seen since leaving Etah. To his joy, he recognized an old friend, paddling his kayak on the search for eider among the islands.

"Paul Zacharias," Petersen cried. "Don't you know me? I'm Carl Petersen."

The man stared at him in fright. "No," he said, "his wife says he's dead," and he paddled off as fast as he could.

Another two days, and a new sound was heard as the men rowed along. It wasn't the gulls; it wasn't the cry of a fox; it was the soft slapping of oars accompanied by a low "halloo!"

"What is it?" Kane asked.

Petersen listened for a moment and then in a trembling half-whisper exclaimed: "*Dannemarkers!*"

The cry echoed again from a nearby cape, then died. Both boats pulled toward it, scanning the shore. Had it all been a dream?

Half an hour passed. Then the single mast of a small shallop showed itself. Petersen began to sob and to cry out, half in English, half in Danish. It was, he said, an Upernavik oil boat. He knew it well: The *Fraulein Flairscher*. "Carlie Mossyn the assistant cooper must be on his road to Kingatok for blubber!"

Petersen was right; in a moment Carlie Mossyn himself appeared. Kane's crew was hungry for news of the outside world, which they had left two years before, and pleaded with Petersen to translate their questions.

"What of America? Eh, Petersen?"

"We don't know much of that country here, for they have no whalers on the coast," said Carlie, "but a steamer and a barque passed up a fortnight ago, and have gone out into the ice to seek your party."

And then he added, as if an afterthought, "Sebastopol ain't taken." That was gibberish to the men, who hadn't heard of the Crimean War between

Great Britain and Russia (1854-56), and the battle to capture that city on the Black Sea.

Now they learned for the first time that the first clues to Franklin's fate—bones of his crew members—had been found a thousand miles (1,600 km) to the southwest. At last Kane realized his searches had been for nothing. Still, he could take heart in his discoveries, for he had moved his ship farther north in the western Arctic than any other white man. He had explored much of the basin that today bears his name. He discovered the largest glacier in the known world. He thought he had "proved" the existence of an Open Polar Sea.

More important, however, was the fact that, through an exercise of willpower, careful planning, and discipline, he had managed on this trek from the ship to bring all but one of his bickering crew through some of the most difficult waters in the world to a safe haven in a friendly Greenland port.

The following night, August 6, 1855, he and his men slept under a civilized roof for the first time since leaving the *Advance*. But after eighty-four days in the open air they did not sleep well, for they were no longer used to civilization.

CHAPTER SEVEN

A National Hero

ELISHA KANE RETURNED TO AMERICA IN THE FALL OF 1855 TO FIND HIMSELF A POPULAR HERO. THE JOURNAL HE HAD WRITTEN DURING THE FIRST EXPEDITION, WITH ITS HAUNTING DESCRIPTIONS OF ICEBERGS AND ITS TERRIFYING ACCOUNT OF BEING TRAPPED IN WELLINGTON CHANNEL, HAD BEEN PUBLISHED WHEN HE WAS AWAY. CONGRESS HAD VOTED ONE HUNDRED AND FIFTY THOUSAND DOLLARS TO SEND TWO SHIPS TO SEARCH FOR HIM.

Luckily, Kane was found at Godhavn after the two search ships, blocked by the ice on Smith Sound, returned to southern Greenland. His younger brother John had accompanied the rescue expedition but didn't recognize the gaunt, bearded creature in the strange, wild costume.

However, by the time the two expeditions reached New York in October, with cannons roaring and crowds cheering, Kane was looking healthier than he had when he left more than two years before. His body had fleshed out, his face was bronze, his neatly-trimmed black beard showed only a touch of grey.

He went straight to the home of his sponsor, Henry Grinnell.

"I have no *Advance* with me," were his first words.

"Never mind," Grinnell told him. "You are safe; that is all we care about. Come into the parlour and tell us the whole story." But Kane never did tell the whole story. His bitterness over what he considered the traitorous actions of his crew, his battles with Godfrey and Blake, his exasperation with Goodfellow and the others, were either left out or toned down in the accounts that followed.

Yet there was still enough on the day after his arrival for the *New York Times* to devote its entire front page to his adventure. The book, on which he worked that winter—his second—sold sixty-five thousand copies, made him a small fortune, and turned him into a national hero.

Although they were based on his own journals, they gave a different picture of the man than the fevered narrative scrawled out in his own hand during the long Arctic nights. The Kane of the best-sellers is a much softer, kindlier man than the Kane revealed in the pages of the journals.

His reputation as a brilliant leader and bold explorer rests almost entirely on the two books. The public and the press of course never saw his personal journal, or that of his sailing master, John Wall Wilson. They had no insight into his flawed leadership, his unruly temperament, his quirky personality, or his towering ego. Wilson tried to write a book of his own but Kane paid him $350 to suppress it.

Kane's best-seller didn't appeal to some of his former shipmates, especially Hayes and Bonsall. They felt he had taken too much of the glory himself. Godfrey wrote an account of his own, but it received little attention. Kane's literary style laid the foundation for his reputation as "the outstanding polar idol of the mid-century."

In truth, he was a better writer than explorer. That is his real contribution to the history of Arctic discovery. It was his graphic tale, prominently displayed on the bookshelves of the nation, that caught the imagination of others and caused them to continue the polar quest.

He was indeed as popular as any modern astronaut, sports hero, or rock star—more popular perhaps, for in those days any man who risked his life in an unknown corner of the world was worshipped far above the common herd. Without films, television, or radio, people depended upon the written word; and here Kane had few equals.

It's important to remember that without Kalutunah and his Inuit comrades, Kane's second voyage would have been a disaster. Indeed, it is doubtful if any of that odd company would have survived without the help of the Natives.

Kane himself adopted many of the Native methods. The igloo he created aboard his ship to survive the winter was certainly based on their own dwellings. Had Franklin and his dying crew paid more attention to Inuit life and practices, it's possible they too might have survived. But the British refused to adopt the Arctic way of life.

Back in New York, there was Kane's romance with Margaret Fox—an object of great interest in the press. She was not in Pennsylvania, where he had sent her. She was back in New York, living with a friend. As soon as he landed in New York, she waited breathlessly for him to call. But she waited in vain.

Margaret could hear the guns heralding the arrival of her lost love. Alas for her, the night passed with no word from him. The following day Henry Grinnell's son, Cornelius, who had been placed in charge of her, arrived to explain that the explorer was ill with rheumatism. He was also concerned about his family and friends, who did not approve of the match with Margaret. Cornelius told her that Kane would come when he was able to. This didn't sound like the same ardent adventurer who had poured out his love to her in a series of letters before vanishing into the Arctic's mists.

In fact, Kane had not mentioned her in his private journal and certainly not in any of his public works. He was a man who had always blown hot and cold, and if he was having second thoughts about Margaret that is not surprising. His family had always exerted a powerful influence upon him and was now in such a state of alarm that they tried to get back the letters he wrote to her.

Kane was torn between his love and respect for his parents and his attachment to Margaret. Forty-eight hours went by after his triumphal arrival. Finally he came to her and an up-and-down relationship continued all winter.

On that first visit she was so overcome she wouldn't see him at first. Then she was in his arms as he showered her with kisses. To her dismay, he told her that any thought of marriage would have to be postponed because of his family's opposition. He said they would be as brother and sister— nothing more. He even forced her to sign a document making such a promise. She did so in tears. Later he sent it back and she tore it up.

Kane had never approved of the séances. He was afraid that Margaret would go back to becoming a spirit rapper. On the other hand, her mother and her sister, Leah, wanted her to return to the stage. She had, after all, been their main source of income.

Both families appeared to be against this marriage. At that, Kane rebelled. He told Margaret his love was stronger than ever. But there is little evidence of that. He himself was dependent on his own family for support until his book was finished. For Margaret that was the end. "I've seen you for the last time," she wrote. "I have been deceived."

At that Kane rushed to her side. He told her that he had betrayed her. "The world shall not say that you, Maggie, are the discarded one!" he cried. "No!—it is you who reject me—Dr. Kane is the discarded lover!" And with that, he threw himself on his knees, pleading, "Speak, Maggie! My destiny is in your hands!"

At least that is the way she described it. For we only have her own account of these events. However, there was undoubtedly some truth in the story. The press was now asking questions, publishing rumours and details, guessing at the possibility of a broken engagement. And so during Kane's trip to New York, they continued to see each other. Then in February, Mrs. Fox forbade him to visit or write to her again. That had little effect.

Meanwhile, he was working furiously on his book. By May 1856, the two-volume work was almost complete. It would run to nine hundred pages. Kane received the coveted gold medal of the Geographical Society of Great Britain.

At about this time, Lady Franklin, who was still stubbornly keeping up her crusade to find her missing husband, appealed to Kane to help in the search. She wanted him to take command of a ship to search for relics of her husband's lost expedition which had been found on King William Island. By this time, however, Kane was too ill to return north.

Lady Franklin would not be put off. She needed him. If he couldn't command a ship, at least he could help her with the campaign to persuade the British to send another expedition to search for the lost men. Kane was tempted. He was certain he could convince the British Admiralty to support the cause. He was also certain that if he totally withdrew from the project it would collapse. Lady Franklin told him she would cross the Atlantic to persuade him, but that wasn't necessary. He decided to go to her.

Undoubtedly he was also tempted by the prospect of the welcome he would receive in Europe. He was an international figure. He knew he would be a great celebrity on the far side of the Atlantic. His book was about to be published. After a few days in England, basking in the celebrations, he planned to go to Switzerland to restore his health.

He was, in fact, very ill. Grinnell said that "he is but a skeleton, or a shadow of one." He made plans to sail in October with his new valet and servant, the faithful William Morton.

He was still seeing Margaret Fox. He took her to the opera, and to the home of friends in New York. She wrote in her memoirs that there was one final ceremony in which the pair entered into a sort of marriage. She said that Kane had spent the evening discussing his health and the possibility that he might die. He feared that she might not come to him if he called. He asked if they might not announce their marriage formally in front of witnesses.

He told her, she said, that that would be "sufficient to constitute a legal marriage," and so she agreed. Four persons, including her mother, were there. Kane took her by the hand, and said: "Maggie is my wife, and I am her husband. Wherever we are, she is mine, and I am hers. Do you understand and consent to this, Maggie?"

She agreed, or so she wrote years later. And from that moment she called herself Mrs. Kane. After all, if he died, she would, as his widow, receive a large sum.

He, himself, was concerned about the future: "Maggie, what if I should die away from you! Oh, my own Maggie, could I but die in your arms, I would ask no more."

It was a wish he could not be granted. He sailed for England on October 11. She never saw him again.

He arrived in London with his heart seriously weakened. He had planned to stay only a few days, then seek a warmer climate. Lady Franklin visited him daily, gave him cod liver oil, brought him books to read. But she continued to act as if he were in command of the search expedition.

He had no intention of taking that on. He was determined to make it clear to her that his determination to withdraw from command a year before was still in force.

A series of dinners, ceremonies, presentations, and other honours kept him longer in England than he had planned. In the end, his doctor persuaded him to visit Cuba where the weather was better. He and Morton left on November 17. Three months later, with his mother and his two brothers at his side, paralyzed by two successive strokes, he died quietly.

The funeral journey that followed was the most spectacular the United

States had ever known, exceeded in that century only by that of Abraham Lincoln. It took a month from Havana, Cuba, to New Orleans, up the Mississippi and Ohio to Cincinnati, and then by train to Philadelphia, the levees and wharfs of the great rivers black with people, the stations in Ohio and Pennsylvania crowded with so many mourners that the tracks were jammed and the train held up.

Bands played, dirges droned, guns boomed, bells tolled, and the air was purple with oratory. At every major river port and whistle-stop the casket came off the train and the body of the "Great Explorer, Ripe Scholar, and Noble Philanthropist" lay in state.

In Philadelphia, seven of Kane's old comrades, including Hayes, Bonsall, Goodfellow, and even Godfrey, followed the bier to Independence Hall, where for three days thousands of mourners filed by.

Kane's ceremonial sword lay on the coffin encircled by a garland of flowers. Only one other tribute lay beside it—a splendid wreath with the message "To the Memory of Dr. Kane from Two Ladies." There was no doubt that the two ladies were the Fox sisters. But Kane himself was one with the spirits. And if from the darkness of his tomb—as cold as the Arctic night—he rapped out a message for posterity, there was none to hear him.

INDEX

A portrait of the triumphant Robert John Le Mesurier McClure,
from his book *The Discovery of the North-West Passage*
by *H.M.S. Investigator*, published in 1857.

(Courtesy Library and Archives Canada, C-087256)

TRAPPED IN THE ARCTIC

CONTENTS

No Way Out

September 1851. For more than a year, Robert McClure, a British naval officer, cut off entirely from the rest of the world, has been exploring the wriggling channels of the western Arctic, discovering new lands that no white man has ever seen. He has already spent one winter frozen in the ice. Now, as he rounds the northern point of Banks Island, the winter again closes in. Just ahead an apparently safe harbour beckons. He manoeuvres his ship through the ice floes into the sheltering bay. Only later does he realize that he is trapped. There is no way out. He cannot get his vessel back over the shoals that block the entrance. Food is running out. Men are dying of scurvy. Two have gone mad. Will he and his six dozen men die by inches, here in this friendless land? Are there any other ships in this vast and lonely realm that may come to his aid? He has no way of knowing. He has unlocked the greatest geographical puzzle of the age: the secret of the North West Passage. But can he survive to bask in that glory? A slow and agonizing death stares him in the face. Only a miracle can save him.

The Mysterious Passage

THE GREAT AGE OF EXPLORATION, WHICH CAPTURED THE IMAGINATION OF OUR ANCESTORS, IS OVER—AT LEAST ON EARTH. ALL THE NOOKS AND CRANNIES OF OUR MODERN WORLD HAVE AT LAST BEEN CHARTED AND MAPPED. WE MUST NOW REACH FOR THE STARS.

But there was a time when the earth held many mysteries and some regions were almost as remote as the moon itself—and almost as difficult to reach. Those who were bold enough and ambitious enough to try achieved a fame even greater than that won by the astronauts of our own age.

In Queen Victoria's time (1837–1901), the great celebrities weren't rock stars, movie idols, or sports figures. They were members of that strange and determined breed of explorers prepared to vanish from civilization for years—to cut off all contact with their wives and families, to face disaster, sickness, even death, to seek the source of the Nile or to unlock the secret of the North West Passage.

The Passage! A century and a half ago there was magic in that word. Since the days of Columbus, seamen had been seeking a shorter route through North and South America—two continents that acted as a barrier between Europe and the treasures of the Orient.

To us this passion seems very strange. Long before 1850, when our story begins, it was clear that even if a passage was found, it would be useless. If it existed at all, it was hidden away in the mists of the Arctic—unknown land that had never been mapped or charted.

Yet the *idea* of such a passage had been so firmly fixed in human minds for some three centuries that it still lured ships and seamen into the frozen world. Men tried to find it, as they sought to reach the summit of Everest— for no practical reason, only because it was there.

It was agreed that whoever found such a passage would be celebrated beyond reason—he would become a heroic figure, showered with wealth, welcomed into the palaces of princes, honoured above all others. Parliament had offered a reward of ten thousand pounds to anyone who could find the Passage—at least half a million dollars in today's money.

For an ambitious explorer in the mid-nineteenth century, the Passage was the greatest of all prizes. This is the story of an ambitious man—ambitious to a fault—who was the first to discover, not *the* Passage, but *a* passage. For, as it turned out, there are several lanes of water wriggling between the Arctic islands, connecting the great Atlantic and Pacific oceans.

Back in the days of Elizabeth I (1558–1603), that old sea dog Martin Frobisher had declared that the discovery of the Passage "is still the only thing left undone."

For the best part of two centuries, British seamen had tried to penetrate the Arctic mystery. If you look at the map of Canada's Arctic, you will see the names of some of these men who explored that vast and forbidding territory—Hudson Bay, Baffin Bay, Davis Strait, Bylot Island—all these commemorate the daring explorers who were the first white men to chart these corners of the frozen world.

Back in the days of Elizabeth I (1558–1603), that old sea dog Martin Frobisher had declared that the discovery of the Passage "is still the only thing left undone, whereby a notable mind might be made famous and remarkable." Frobisher made three voyages between 1576 and 1578 on a vain quest for the elusive channel.

Others followed. In 1585 John Davis rediscovered Greenland, which had been forgotten after the failure of the Norse colonies three centuries before, but he didn't find the Passage.

Henry Hudson sailed through the strait that bears his name in 1610. Bursting into a seemingly limitless sea, he thought he had succeeded in reaching the Pacific. He was wrong. In fact he had discovered Hudson Bay—which would immortalize his name, but only after he met his death at the hands of a mutinous crew.

In 1616 Hudson's pilot, Robert Bylot, and his brilliant sidekick, William Baffin, left their names on two Arctic islands, travelling three hundred miles

(480 km) farther north than any white man before them. But they didn't find the Passage.

When Luke Foxe reported in 1631 that there could be no route to the Orient south of the Arctic Circle, he killed all hope of a practical passage. That slowed down the search, but didn't end it.

The Arctic still remained a blank on the map, except for parts of Henry Hudson's vast bay and Bylot and Baffin's great Arctic islands.

Two overland explorers managed to reach the Arctic waters. Samuel Hearne arrived at the mouth of the Coppermine River in 1771, and Alexander Mackenzie reached the delta of the river named for him in 1789. The Arctic itself remained a mystery.

After the end of the Napoleonic Wars in 1815, the search for the Passage began again. One may well ask why. The fact is that, with the world at peace, the Royal Navy had to find work for its officers, 90 percent of whom had nothing to do.

For an ambitious man like Robert McClure, there was little chance for promotion. There were just too many officers. In fact at one point there was one naval officer in Great Britain for every three sailors! Only by performing some impossible and miraculous feat could a man like McClure hope to gain promotion.

And so, with nothing to lose but their lives, and with an overabundance of sea-going craft anchored in the harbours, the men of the Royal Navy launched a new age of exploration.

In those days the Canadian North was almost entirely unknown. We know it now from photographs, illustrations, films, and travellers' accounts. If we have the fare we can board a plane and fly all the way to the Arctic Ocean. People live in the Arctic and are in touch by radio and TV. But in McClure's time, the Arctic was inaccessible to outsiders. The explorers of the nineteenth century were cut off totally.

The Royal Navy sent ship after ship into the Arctic seeking the Passage. Ship after ship returned, often after its crew endured fearful hardships, with nothing to report. One such crew, under Sir John Ross, actually spent five years cut off from civilization. Given up for lost, Ross returned at last in the summer of 1833, having wrecked one of his two vessels. But he had not found what he had been seeking.

In 1845 another expedition was launched to search for the Passage. Its leader was a rather ordinary, but very likeable seaman named John Franklin. In his sixtieth year, he was far too old to attempt such a feat, but the British Admiralty let him go anyway, because he wanted the prize so badly.

Franklin and his 129 men vanished into the Arctic mists and were never seen alive again by their countrymen. His two stubby little vessels, *Erebus* and *Terror*, were never found, though not for lack of trying. It was maddening! Somewhere in that maze of bald islands and wriggling channels, there *must* be some clues to Franklin's fate. But for years not a single clue could be found.

And so the search for the Passage was joined by a parallel search for Franklin and his men. Now there were two prizes dangled before the ambitious young men seeking fame and fortune. All of England wanted both mysteries solved.

It is difficult today to understand the wave of emotion and despair that washed over Great Britain when, in 1848, it became obvious that Franklin and his men were lost and probably dead. Public prayers were said in sixty churches for the safety of the expedition. Fifty thousand well-wishers attended.

That year the Royal Navy launched an ambitious three-pronged attack that would see one overland party and four ships explore the maze of islands and channels from three directions—east, west, and south.

For eighteen months these expeditions were out of touch with the world, and when they returned they had no shred of news concerning the missing men—no clues, no messages, *nothing*. One expedition made a remarkable seven-hundred-mile (1,126-km) journey in small boats along the northern Alaska coast from the Bering Sea to the Mackenzie Delta, and returned empty-handed—establishing beyond doubt that Franklin had not gone west to that great river. In November of 1849, the two other expeditions limped back to England to report failure. One of them was commanded by a famous Antarctic explorer, Sir James Ross (a nephew of John Ross). It arrived home with six of the company of sixty-four dead, another twelve sick, and the commander's own health broken.

A kind of Arctic fever swept England. Books about polar journeys, huge paintings showing Arctic scenes, newspaper and magazine articles about northern adventure, all combined to stimulate the public to a fever pitch.

The British Navy decided to enlarge the search. Because James Ross had been blocked in Barrow Strait—in the eastern Arctic—by impassible ice conditions, the Navy, in the fall of 1849, turned its attention to the west. If ships couldn't pierce the unknown Arctic core from the east, perhaps they could enter the Arctic Ocean from Bering Strait in the west and proceed eastward.

Ross's two ships, *Enterprise* and *Investigator,* were available. An expedition was quickly outfitted. Captain Richard Collinson in the *Enterprise* would be its leader, and Lieutenant Robert McClure, who had been with Ross on the previous expedition, would be second-in-command, and in charge of the *Investigator.*

The two ships left Plymouth on January 20. This was only the first of six expeditions that would set off that year to search for John Franklin.

None of these searches were successful. But this great sweep of the mysterious Arctic, which continued for years, was not without its side benefits. Franklin had been sent to search for the fabled North West Passage. The searchers did not find Franklin himself, but they found the Passage and explored the maze of Arctic islands. And the man who got the credit was Collinson's second-in-command, Lieutenant Robert McClure.

The story of McClure and his voyage is the story of a man prepared to risk the lives of himself and his crew in order to achieve his ambition. But it is also the story of the opening up of a channel from west to east in the great maze of naked islands that lies to the north of the mainland of Canada. These islands are now part of Canada, largely because of people like Franklin, McClure, and many other British seamen who were the first white men to see them.

VICTORIA
ISLAND

(Wollaston
Land)

CHAPTER ONE

The Explorer and the Missionary

LET US JOIN ROBERT MCCLURE AS HE STRIDES THE FOREDECK OF THE
INVESTIGATOR—A HANDSOME MAN WITH A HAWK'S NOSE, AN UNRULY SHOCK
OF BLACK HAIR, AND A FRINGE OF CHIN WHISKERS JOINED TO HIS LONG SIDE-
BURNS.

On the horizon he can spot his sister ship, the *Enterprise*, under his
superior, Richard Collinson. The Royal Navy never sends a single ship on
such an expedition. Its vessels are to travel in pairs so that, in the event of
disaster—and there have been many disasters—one ship can go to the aid
of the other, and, if necessary, take her crew aboard.

Later events suggest that McClure was not entirely happy with this
arrangement. He had two goals in mind, either of which would set him up
for life. He would find Franklin and, in finding Franklin, he would also find
the fabled Passage. He was not one to share this triumph with a fellow officer, especially one like the peppery Collinson, who outranked him. He
wanted all the glory for himself.

He faced a long and difficult voyage. It would take his ship from the
British Isles to the tip of South America, around Cape Horn, and then
across the Pacific to the Sandwich Islands (which we call Hawaii). The two
ships would then sail north and west in a great circle around the long finger
of the Aleutian Island chain that reaches almost to Asia. Having skirted the
Aleutians, they would then head northeast again to the northern coast of
Alaska, which belonged to Russia in the mid-1800s.

That journey would add up to more than 25,000 miles (40,233 km)—a
distance equal to the circumference of Earth. When he reached Point
Barrow on Alaska's Arctic coast, McClure would, at last, be at the entrance
to the western Arctic. At the same time, far to the east, other ships, British

and American, would also be searching for Franklin. The frozen world had never known such activity.

McClure is a fascinating character. He had spent twenty-six years in the Navy, but this was his first command and he intended to make the most of it. He knew that if he could either find Franklin or discover the Passage he would be the most famous man in England, as well as the richest naval officer of his day. Although most Arctic explorers were ambitious, McClure's ambition was more naked and less admirable. There is little doubt that McClure was out for McClure first, and everybody else second.

Although he made important discoveries, he was not generous enough to share his triumphs with others. Yet we must admire his daring. He took big chances and he won, even though he put his crew and himself in danger. And, like most successful explorers, he had his share of luck and knew how to make the most of it.

> *Although most Arctic explorers were ambitious, McClure's ambition was more naked and less admirable. There is little doubt that McClure was out for McClure first, and everybody else second.*

But it is also clear that McClure was unstable. He suffered spasms of uncontrollable fury when the progress of his expedition—and thus his own ambitions—was threatened.

He had waited a long time for this command. He came from an Army, not a Navy background. He was educated at the best places, Eton and Sandhurst, and joined the Navy quite late for a young Englishman—at the age of seventeen. (Many a young midshipman joined at the age of thirteen.) He had served on two previous Arctic expeditions. The first, in 1836, was disastrous. The second, in 1848, when he was a lieutenant under James Clark Ross, gave him more experience.

He was not comfortable in command. He kept to himself and was not an easy man to know. He didn't care much for his own officers, who were young, inexperienced, and often slovenly. Many, in fact, were incompetent. And his crew was unruly and often sullen.

McClure really didn't know how to deal with them as many other commanders did. He flogged his men unmercifully for minor breaches of discipline. His cook, for instance, was given forty-eight lashes for swearing.

Yet, though he often put his own fierce ambitions ahead of his crew's safety, in moments of real danger he had the ability to gather his men together and rally them with a few words.

Unlike his predecessor, Edward Parry, he made no attempt to lessen the boredom of an Arctic winter. Parry had brought along a magic lantern, arranged for theatrical performances, and even published a newspaper to keep his crew mentally healthy. McClure's men were left largely to their own devices.

Still, he managed to survive through four winters—from 1850 to 1854—with very little of the discord that marked so many other Arctic voyages. He did this partly through tough discipline, but also because in a tight spot he was able to rouse his men to superhuman effort.

It wasn't in Robert McClure's makeup to be on friendly terms with his officers. His closest companion, oddly enough, was a civilian, Johann August Miertsching. Miertsching was a Moravian missionary from Labrador who had been brought along because he spoke the native tongue and could act as an interpreter. Perhaps because he was a civilian, McClure felt Miertsching could in some way relax the formality that he thought proper to his command.

Miertsching, a pious young evangelist, was thirty-two years old and a favourite of everybody. Strong, cheerful, never in a bad temper, he had been long accustomed to the conditions of Labrador, which were similar to those of the Arctic. And unlike the British sailors who dressed in their wool uniforms, he wore Inuit clothing. He also got along well with McClure. The fairest descriptions we have of the expedition came from his own accounts.

Following their departure from Plymouth, the *Enterprise* and the *Investigator* sailed down the east coast of North and South America to the Straits of Magellan at the very tip. The fog was so thick it was obvious they couldn't stay together, so Collinson arranged with McClure to meet off Cape Lisburne, on the west coast of Alaska.

Now McClure was on his own. His first port of call would be Honolulu in the Hawaiian Islands. But the voyage wasn't happy. Miertsching especially, who had no experience of life aboard a British warship, was shocked by the crew, whom he thought insolent and godless. "I feel as if my lot had been cast among half a hundred devils," he wrote. "The harsh rules of naval discipline are barely enough to keep them under control."

This was the year of the California Gold Rush. Ships loaded with adventurers were racing for the west coast. The *Investigator*, having rounded Cape Horn, was on a different tack, heading directly for Hawaii through weather so dreadful that seventeen of the crew were sick.

Then, on May 15, the ship was almost lost. McClure's first officer, William Haswell, had left the deck for a few minutes, and in that brief time a squall struck the ship a dreadful blow, smashing all three masts.

McClure flew into a fury—"the most unpleasant that I have yet experienced," according to Miertsching. The captain put his first officer under arrest for his neglect. After that his anger subsided as quickly as it had arisen.

Later, McClure seemed to regret this moment of ungovernable fury, which Miertsching described as "positively inhuman." When the missionary fell ill, McClure took him into his cabin and poured out his apologies. He seemed to regret "that he had forgotten himself and had not handled the affair as a sincere Christian should have done."

But McClure himself was not particularly religious. "At sea," he told the missionary, "a man must have experience and not hang his head." He told Miertsching he was not yet a true seaman, and described a naval officer he once knew who had tried to practise "land Christianity" aboard a man-of-war. "He learned by experience that it did not serve on board a ship; so he gave up the sea, and became a parson and wrote tracts for old wives."

McClure scoffed at the missionary's practice of handing out religious tracts to the crew. He'd do better, he said, to give them to "loose women," who would receive them with more thanks than the sailors did. But the day would come when the Arctic would shake McClure out of his cynicism, as it shook so many others.

CHAPTER TWO

A Daring Gamble

THE *INVESTIGATOR* REACHED HONOLULU HARBOUR ON JULY 1, 1850. NOW, TO HIS ALARM, MCCLURE LEARNED THAT COLLINSON, HIS SUPERIOR, HAD LINGERED FOUR DAYS AND THEN DECIDED TO WAIT NO LONGER. HE HAD SET SAIL THE PREVIOUS MORNING FOR BERING STRAIT, WHICH SEPARATES ALASKA AND SIBERIA. THIS HASTY DEPARTURE, AS WE SHALL SEE, DOOMED COLLINSON TO A MINOR POSITION IN THE LIST OF ARCTIC HEROES.

Collinson had left word that if McClure didn't catch up he would head east at once into the maze of the Arctic islands. The British supply ship *Plover*, which had been anchored in the strait since 1849, would go with him.

That was too much for McClure. Was he to be denied his chance at fame and fortune? He was in a frenzy to get moving. He had planned to get rid of some of his officers, especially Haswell, who was still under arrest. But now every hour counted. He allowed Haswell to make a suitable apology and signed him on again.

In a perfect whirlwind of activity, he worked around the clock to get his ship loaded with provisions and to round up his crew members. Many had celebrated so well that they were now in jail in Honolulu. He paid their fines, but found they were not fit for duty. It must have been a colossal bender! Two weeks later, several were still on the sick list, not yet recovered from what Miertsching called "the frightful excesses in Honolulu."

McClure managed to get his men rounded up and his ship into shape in just three days. At six o'clock, on the evening of July 4, he left the tropical Hawaiian waters behind and headed north to the Arctic. He had decided upon a daring, but dangerous gamble. He wouldn't just catch up with Collinson. He would beat him to Cape Lisburne on the northwest tip of

Alaska! Then he would try to get ahead of him, in what was now turning out to be a race for the western Arctic.

The expedition had been ordered to circle around the outer islands of the Aleutian chain. That would take them close to the Kamchatka Peninsula of Asia. That was the way Collinson had gone. This long, 1,100-mile (1,770-km) finger of volcanic islands was a mystery. No one had charted it. Masked by a thick cloak of fog, the Aleutians were subject to violent tides, which swept over shoals and reefs that could cause an unwary captain to wreck his ship. McClure decided on a bold and dangerous gamble: he would take a huge shortcut through this dangerous island chain, cutting through them at the eastern end.

The gamble succeeded. McClure reached Kotzebue Sound just south of Cape Lisburne on July 29. The journey had taken just twenty-five days— half the time it would have taken to sail around the Aleutians.

Kotzebue Sound lies at the northern limits of the Bering Strait, and there McClure spied the British depot ship, *Plover*. There was no sign, of

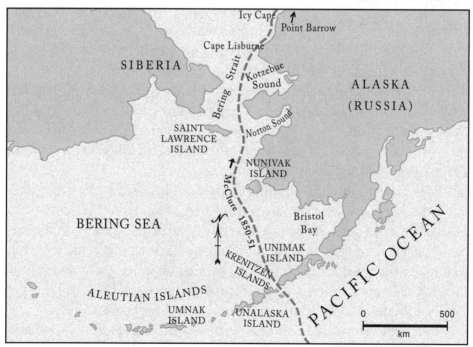

McClure's route to Alaska, 1850

155

the rendezvous point at Cape Lisburne. On the way he was hailed by another Royal Navy vessel, the frigate *Herald*, commanded by Captain Henry Kellett, whose job it was to keep the *Plover* supplied with provisions.

At this point McClure engaged in a bald deception—which did not fool Kellett, an experienced commander. McClure pretended to believe that Collinson had gone on *ahead* of him. That, of course, was impossible. Kellett knew how long it would take to get around the Aleutian Islands. Collinson, he reckoned, must be at least twenty days behind McClure.

Yet here was McClure proposing to enter the dangerous Arctic without any escort vessel. The orders had been quite clear: the two ships were supposed to stick together. McClure ignored those instructions. He pretended he was actually trying to follow the Navy's instruction by catching up with his superior!

The Investigator shuddered and almost came to a stop. The masts trembled so violently they seemed about to shake the ship to pieces.

Kellett, who outranked him, could have stopped him. In fact he tried. But he was reluctant to give a direct order. McClure kept up the pretence—even kept some personal mail for Collinson, which he said he would deliver when they met. But of course they never did meet.

Kellett tried to get him to wait at least forty-eight hours. McClure refused. In fact, he all but dared the senior officer to stop him—and that Kellett wouldn't do. The British Navy had not figured on this. There were no instructions as to what should be done if the ships failed to meet off the Alaska coast. And so Kellett let McClure go.

Away he went into the grinding confusion of the ice pack. A tongue of ice, solid as granite, blocked his way. With a wind behind him, McClure ordered up every shred of canvas, then boldly turned his prow into the very centre of the mass. The *Investigator* shuddered and almost came to a stop. The masts trembled so violently they seemed about to shake the ship to pieces. Then the ice split under the force of the blow, and they were through into open water. McClure had won the second of his gambles.

Now, with the wind against her, the *Investigator* would have to be towed around Point Barrow at the northwest tip of Alaska. That took forty men in five boats, pulling on the oars until they were exhausted. That task completed, they entered unknown waters. Ninety miles (144 km) to the north, the captain could see the permanent polar ice pack—a stupendous, glittering wall of white, centuries old. He had never seen anything like that before in the eastern Arctic.

His ship groped her way along the northern coast of Alaska, often moving up blind channels and returning to the main one, sometimes trapped in the ice for hours, even days. At last McClure passed the great Mackenzie Delta. He was seeking Banks Island, which Parry, the first of the Arctic explorers, had spotted in the distance years before.

This was unknown country. Many of the Natives whom they met had never seen a white man. McClure and his officers worried about their souls and their lack of civilization, for they believed that every Native should become a Christian.

Now the man who had dismissed the idea of Christianity, in his talk with the Labrador missionary, wrote that he hoped "some practically Christian body … could send a few of their brethren amongst the tribes … to carry to them the arts and advantages of civilized life, and trust in God, in his own good time, showing them the way to eternal life." It did not occur to McClure, or indeed to any other officer of the Royal Navy, that there were many forms of life, civilized and otherwise, which were just as cultured and accomplished as those McClure knew.

The attitude to the Inuit, who in those days were known as Eskimos, was at best patronizing, and at worst racist. The ship's doctor, Alexander Armstrong, thought them "the most filthy race on the face of the globe … thieving, cunning … treacherous and deceitful …" He trusted that "the day is not far distant when the light of civilization will dawn on this poor, benighted but intelligent race of human beings." He thought that the Hudson's Bay Company had made no effort to remove them from what he called "a state of heathen darkness."

The Natives were equally bewildered by the white men. They thought the ship had been carved out of a single, enormous tree, and wanted to know where such trees grew. Community property was part of their way of life, and so they thought nothing of taking any object they wanted. One enterprising man even went so far as to slip his hand into McClure's pocket, while a woman tried to conceal a large anvil by hiding it under her, like a hen sitting on an egg. This misunderstanding of their views confirmed the British in their belief that the Inuit were an immoral lot, desperately in need of divine guidance.

At Cape Bathurst, northeast of the Mackenzie Delta, the Inuit were enchanted by Miertsching, who spoke their language, wore clothes like theirs, and told them wonderful and exciting tales about a great good spirit who had created the sun, moon, stars, rocks, and water. They accepted it all with amazement and wonder. They had their own concept of heaven and hell, remarkably like the Christian one—a good land with a good spirit who looked after animals so they didn't disappear from the land, and a bad land with a bad spirit who did great harm. They believed that each person who died would be sent to the destination he had earned in life.

Miertsching was beginning to love these simple, cheerful people. He didn't want to leave them. In fact, their chief pleaded with him to stay and tell him more of his marvellous stories, even offering his sixteen-year-old daughter as his bride. A throng followed him to the beach where fifteen kayaks paddled off to the ship to bid him farewell. But Miertsching, too, worried about their souls.

Miertsching could not stay, much as he might have wanted to. The ice was already gathering along the shore. Winter was settling in. Ahead lay the unknown, and somewhere hidden in that glittering, frozen mass lay Franklin's missing ships. Was it too much to hope that somewhere, too, in that maze of friendless islands, was to be found the elusive Passage?

CHAPTER THREE

The Passage at Last

THE *INVESTIGATOR* SLOWLY SAILED EAST BETWEEN THE GATHERING MASSES OF ICE. THE LAND ON THE RIGHT BEGAN TO RISE UNTIL, ON THE WESTERN SIDE OF FRANKLIN BAY, THE CLIFFS SOARED TO SEVEN HUNDRED FEET (213 M). MCCLURE TRIED TO KEEP GOING, BUT THE ICE BLOCKED HIS WAY. HE WAS FORCED NORTH IN A ZIGZAG COURSE TOWARD A LOFTY, MOUNTAINOUS LAND OF DIZZY CLIFFS, BACKED BY TWO-THOUSAND-FOOT (610-M) PEAKS.

There, on August 7, under a towering mass of rock that he named Lord Nelson Head (after the famous British admiral who was killed in 1805), McClure planted a flag and took possession of the territory. He named it Baring Land, after the first lord of the British Admiralty. He didn't know yet that he had actually landed on Banks Island, which he had been trying to reach ever since leaving Point Barrow.

Luck was on his side. He was imprisoned by the moving ice and couldn't even move around the southern shore of the new land. The ice was totally in charge, driving him steadily northward, up a narrow channel that followed the eastern shore of the island. He had no idea as to whether this was a dead end or not. If it was a strait, it might indeed be part of the North West Passage.

On September 9, he was just sixty miles (96 km) from the western end of Barrow Strait. That meant he was only sixty miles from territory that had already been explored. Here was the final gap to connect the east and the west.

McClure could not contain his excitement. "I cannot describe my anxious feelings," he wrote. "Can it be possible that this water communicates with Barrow's Strait, and shall be the long sought North West Passage? Can it be that so humble a creature as I am will be permitted to perform what has baffled the talented and wise for hundreds of years!" He praised God for having brought him so far without mishap. But he didn't mention the main object of his search. John Franklin's name does not occur at this point in his journal.

But he could go no farther. On September 17, young ice forming in front of him made it impossible to continue. He had come as far as he could that season. Now he had a decision to make. Should he try to find an anchorage farther south in some sheltered bay? Or should he allow his ship to become frozen in?

A lookout in the crow's nest—nothing more than a barrel attached to the top of the mast—could see twenty miles (32 km) to the north. In the distance the land tapered off to the northeast and the northwest leaving a clear expanse of water beyond. Now McClure knew he was on the edge of a great discovery. For Barrow Strait lay ahead, and beyond that, Melville Island. That had been explored by Sir Edward Parry thirty years before. In short, the last link in the North West Passage was in sight.

McClure was determined to stay in the pack ice. He knew it was dangerous, but he hadn't come this far to turn back.

McClure was determined to stay in the pack ice. He knew it was dangerous, but he hadn't come this far to turn back. He had no intention of giving up the ground he had gained.

He had expected to be trapped in the ice, but instead he was caught in the moving pack. A dreadful gale, blowing down the channel, forced the ice south, and with it his ship, which was anchored to a vast floe. Like an unhorsed rider in a cattle stampede, McClure was helpless.

The *Investigator* was carried directly back the way she had come. For more than a week, she was in daily peril. She was swept thirty miles (48 km) south, then whirled about and forced north again. Now she was in danger of being crushed against the cliffs of the newly discovered Princess Royal Islands in the middle of the Prince of Wales Strait.

On September 26, McClure was prepared to abandon ship. He ordered a year's provisions stacked on the deck, ready to be thrown into the boats if the ship went down. The men stood by with bundles of warm clothes, their pockets stuffed with ammunition for hunting, and biscuits to eat.

If necessary they were prepared to leap from the ship and try to struggle to the shore across the grinding ice.

The following night was even worse. They kept a seventeen-hour vigil, and during that time huge bergs, some of them three times as big as the ship, crashed against its sides until the oakum that was used for caulking squeezed from the seams.

Convinced they were doomed, the seamen abandoned all discipline. They broke open casks of liquor on deck and became roaring drunk. As the ship was flung over on her side, an enormous heap of crushed ice threatened to bury her and all the sixty-six men aboard. Then, miraculously, the gale died and the ship righted herself.

What had happened to save them? The explanation was simple enough. It was so cold that the rampaging ice had been frozen into a solid, unmoving sheet. Exhausted and limp, shocked into silence, the drenched and drunken sailors tried to grab some rest. The pressure had been so great that ropes nine inches (23 cm) thick had been snapped like threads, tearing all six ice anchors away.

With the storm over and two feet (61 cm) of water pumped out of the hold, McClure, who had scarcely spoken a word since the turmoil, mustered his crew and coldly read out the Articles of War regarding ship's discipline. He followed this with a savage tongue-lashing in which he called them a band of thieves, unworthy of the name of Englishmen. He was ashamed, he said, that such a rabble should walk the decks of a British ship. He promised that those who had opened the casks of liquor would be punished. Then he relented and reminded his men of the miracle that had saved them. Human strength had been ineffective; almighty Providence had preserved them from certain death. His words brought tears to the eyes of the most hardened seamen, who cheered their captain and promised to mend their ways.

The terrible trial that all had gone through had sobered both the men and the officers. McClure was now the commander of a happier ship. He himself took to reading the Bible, morning and night. As Miertsching put it, "he seems now to realize that he is not the good exemplary Christian which he used to think himself."

It was now October 1850. At this point, some five hundred miles (800 km) to the northeast, eight British ships lay frozen into the ice of Barrow

Strait. In addition, two American vessels had been trapped in the moving ice pack in Wellington Channel. Of course, McClure had no way of knowing that. With his own ship sealed, covered, and protected by a vast wall of ice, he turned his attention again to the North West Passage.

McClure had to be absolutely sure that the water the lookout in the crow's nest had seen in the distance really was a continuation of Barrow Strait. And so, on October 10, he took a sledge party across the ice to the land on the east side of the frozen channel. He named it Prince Albert Land, after Queen Victoria's husband. Actually it was a peninsula of the vast Victoria Island.

Accompanied by Dr. Armstrong and a few companions, McClure struggled up a fifteen-hundred-foot (457-m) mountain, panting from the unaccustomed exercise. From that vantage point, he saw in the distance the end of the ice-packed channel that he had named Prince of Wales Strait. The doctor was convinced that "the highway to England from ocean to ocean lay before us." That wasn't good enough for McClure. He himself would have to set foot on the shore of the Passage.

Eleven days later he led another sledge party on a second exhausting journey along the eastern shore of Banks Island to the end of the channel. And there, five days later—October 26, 1850, a fine, cloudless day—Robert McClure, standing on a six-hundred-foot (183-m) neck of land, finally confirmed that he had reached the water route from Atlantic to Pacific.

"Thank God!" one of his crewmen muttered, as the sunrise brightened to reveal the land ahead curving off to the north toward a strait that would be named for McClure and to the southeast toward Melville Sound. Obviously the Passage was useless. Prince of Wales Strait was blocked, and no ship was ever likely to force its way through the ice stream by this route. That didn't matter to McClure. Nor did it matter that though he had seen the Passage from afar, he hadn't conquered it. He knew now his name would go down in the history books as the man who had made the greatest sea-going discovery of the age.

It was just as well he did not know then that some of John Franklin's men had found another North West Passage two years earlier. In the years that followed, the public would favour the more popular explorer. But nobody could take away from Robert McClure this moment of triumph.

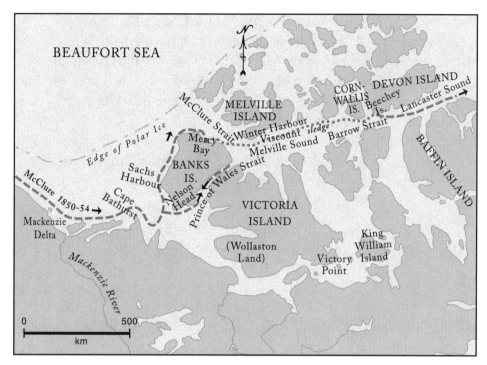

BEAUFORT SEA

MELVILLE ISLAND

CORN- DEVON ISLAND
WALLIS
IS. Beechey
IS. Lancaster Sound

McClure Strait

Winter Harbour

Viscount sledge
Melville Sound
Barrow Strait

Edge of Polar Ice

Mercy Bay

BANKS IS.

Sachs Harbour

Prince of Wales Strait

BAFFIN ISLAND

McClure 1850-54 →

Cape Bathurst

Nelson Head

VICTORIA ISLAND

King William Island

(Wollaston Land)

Victory Point

Mackenzie Delta

Mackenzie River

0   500
km

McClure's discovery of a North West Passage, 1850–54

Dr. Armstrong confessed to "an indescribable feeling of pride and pleasure" at the thought that "the maritime greatness and glory of our country were still further elevated above all nations of the earth; the solution of this great enigma leaving nothing undone to confirm Great Britain's Queen—Empress of the Sea …"

That was laying it on pretty thick. Even the Inuit didn't bother to go that far north. What the search for the elusive Passage had accomplished was to so concentrate the British on northern exploration that by the end of the century the entire Arctic would be mapped and the waters charted.

McClure got back to his ship October 31. He was thin and exhausted, having rushed on ahead of his crew, lost his way, and wandered about without sleep for an entire Arctic night. He was taken on board unable to speak, his limbs stiff with cold, looking more like a corpse than a living human being.

Two days later he formally told his crew about his discovery. They would share in the reward that had been offered for finding the Passage. He told them he hoped they would be home with their families within a year. For that they gave him three hearty cheers, three more for the Queen, three for the discovery, three more for the rest of the officers, and three for their sweethearts and wives. They followed that with one final cheer, and everybody got grog and extra meat for supper.

In victory, McClure was unusually humble. "The world may speak of me or the ship as having done this but a higher power than me has directed us," he said. The sledge journey had exhausted him and for the next month he was confined to his cot.

VICTORIA
ISLAND

(Wollaston
Land)

CHAPTER FOUR

Mercy Bay

McClure hadn't quite forgotten that the main object of the expedition was to search for John Franklin. He sent out three sledge journeys the following spring. With these he also hoped to solve several geographical puzzles. He wanted to know which lands he had discovered were attached to the land mass of North America and which were islands.

The sledgers didn't get away until April 1851. They were not enthusiastic about these journeys. The harbour was not sheltered, and the *Investigator* was in a dangerous position in the very middle of Prince of Wales Strait, which was still frozen. Most of the men who left thought themselves doomed. They didn't expect to find the ship in one piece when they got back.

McClure knew that there would be a terrible upheaval when the ice broke. He had already placed a depot on one of the Princess Royal Islands with three months' provisions in case the ship should be crushed by the rampaging ice. If that happened, he hoped they might be able to travel toward the Mackenzie Delta by small boat or sledge and then go up that river to the nearest trading post. But that was a long shot at best.

With the threat of shipwreck hanging over them, the tensions among the crew and officers returned. One sledge party was told to follow the south shore of Melville Sound toward Cape Walker. Unfortunately, its captain, Robert Wynniatt, broke his chronometer (a naval timepiece) a week after he left. He used this as an excuse to hurry back to the ship. McClure thought he had come back with news of Franklin and flew into a rage when he learned the real reason. He sent Wynniatt back immediately without a new chronometer—an absurd and senseless act.

Lieutenant Samuel Cresswell's party, which was sent to explore the northeast coast of Banks Island, also came back a week early. Two men were suffering from frostbite, and another had to have part of his foot amputated. Those who weren't disabled were sent out again after only two days' rest to chart the south shore of Banks Island. That was another harsh decision by McClure.

He was bitterly disappointed that none of the parties had managed either to find Franklin or to fulfil their other assignments. In fact, he would have been even angrier had he known that Wynniatt's party at one point was just a few miles from one of the sledges from a ship sent out to search for Franklin from the east.

There was one journey that McClure could have made that he neglected—it was a failure that would cause untold hardships. Only a hundred miles (160 km) to the north was Sir Edward Parry's old winter camp on Melville Island. Parry had left a cairn there, and it was more than likely that the searchers from the other end of the Arctic would visit it. If McClure had left a message at Parry's cairn, they would know where he was. In truth, one party did visit the cairn, seeking just such a message, and found nothing. McClure's neglect doomed him to spend three more winters in the Arctic.

The three sledge journeys turned up nothing. McClure tried again. A hundred miles (160 km) south, on the shores of Prince Albert Land, the party under Lieutenant Haswell had discovered a new band of Inuit. McClure had decided now to seek these people out in hopes that they could tell him something about the lost Franklin expedition.

Off he went at a cracking pace, taking six men and Miertsching, the missionary. There, on June 2, he reached the tents of the Natives, and there, to his astonishment, an Inuit woman drew an almost perfect chart of the area on the paper he supplied. It showed the entire coastline of North America, which none of the Natives had ever visited, and it filled up blanks on the existing maps. The Inuit, as other explorers had already learned, were expert map-makers.

The Inuit were astonished to learn that there were other lands inhabited by human beings. McClure found them both friendly and intelligent. Their simple habits brought out in him an unexpected tenderness, and when it came time to depart, Miertsching noted that "the captain was so grieved at leaving these loving people helpless in this frightful region of ice that he could not refrain from tears."

A touching little scene followed. In a sudden gesture, McClure took off his thick red shawl and wound it around the neck of a young woman who was standing nearby with a child on her back. She was startled. The idea of gift giving was foreign to these people. It was part of their code always to offer something of equal value in return, but she had nothing to give him. And so she took the baby out from under her hood, covered it with kisses, and, in a remarkable gesture, offered it to McClure in exchange.

Miertsching had difficulty explaining that his captain wasn't proposing a trade. She understood at last and, laughing, accepted the shawl, which until then she had refused to touch. She wanted to know what animal it was that had a red skin. But there was no time to explain. One of the men was already suffering badly from frostbite, and McClure wanted to get back to the ship.

It is ironic that McClure, who showed a good deal of pity and concern for the Inuit, believed that, by Christianizing and "civilizing" them, he could better their condition. We know now that this attitude led only to a disruption of the Native way of life, to infection by European diseases, and to the destruction of a value system that had worked perfectly well until the two peoples met each other. The exploration of the Arctic islands, hailed as a great achievement by the white European community, brought little but misery to the people whose lands were invaded.

Six weeks later, on July 14, the ice in Prince of Wales Strait broke up without incident. McClure headed back north hoping to skip through the North West Passage and complete the trip from Pacific to Atlantic. That, as it turned out, was not possible. The great ice stream that pours down from the north barred his way, as it had barred the way of other explorers.

On August 16, McClure made a sudden decision. He would sail south again and try to circle around Baring (or Banks) Land (in fact Banks Island). If it was an island, then he could get into the waters connected to Barrow Strait from the far side and still make his way through the famous Passage.

This was another daring, even foolhardy gamble. It was late in the year. McClure knew nothing of the fogbound, ice-choked channel he was planning to enter. He was chancing an encounter with what Miertsching correctly called "the frightful polar pack." He was risking his ship and the lives of his crew. He had discovered the Passage, he had searched vainly for Franklin, he could have gone back the way he had come. But McClure was a man obsessed. He had seen the Passage, but he had not sailed through it. He didn't want half the glory; he wanted it all.

He was astonished to find the channel to the south was free of ice. He sped down it in a single day, rounding Nelson Head with a fresh breeze spurring him on. By August 18 he had covered three hundred miles (480 km) without being held up by ice.

The white world came alive. Polar bears lumbered over the shore ice. Caribou pounded across the barren slopes. Seals basked in the sunshine. Geese, wild swans, and ducks rose in flocks from the water.

On the southwest corner of Banks Land, on what is now known as Sachs Harbour, he left a note in a cairn for his missing commander, Collinson, who found it three weeks later. But the two never met up with one another.

Meanwhile, McClure's luck continued to hold. He rounded the southwest cape of Banks Land and scudded north at speeds as high as seven knots (13 km/h). For a day he travelled up a broad lane of water created by the polar pack on his left and the island on his right. Then the lane began to narrow. The land rose. The pack drew closer, until it seemed they were in a kind of a canyon with high cliffs of ice on one side, rising a hundred feet (30 m) out of the sea, and the dizzier cliffs of rock towering above him on the other.

The *Investigator* was so close to the land that her boats had to be hauled up to prevent them from being smashed against the rock walls. By the time the ship stood off Cape Prince Alfred at the northwest corner of Banks Island, the channel wasn't any more than two hundred feet (60 m) wide. The crews had to take to the boats to tow the ship past the cliffs, blasting at them with black powder.

On August 20 the ship came to a halt with the ice pressing on her. Shore parties explored the headland and came upon an ancient forest—masses of petrified trees piled on hills and in gorges. Some of them had trunks ten inches (25 cm) thick, but now they had been turned to stone. Here was proof that this frozen land had once been a warm region with a thick forest and smiling meadows.

Now the Arctic returned to attack with all its fury. Again, the men were ordered on deck with their belongings, ready to leave at any instant. The high spring tide and the west wind hurled masses of ice down on the ship, again throwing her broadside against the floe to which she was anchored.

Beams cracked, doors sprang open. "This is the end!" McClure cried, "The ship is breaking up; in five minutes she will be sunk." He was about to cut the cables that attached them to the ice floe, when another miracle occurred. The ice suddenly became motionless.

By this time McClure was convinced a Higher Power was shielding him, that no lives would be lost, and that all would get back to their homes safely. His pale and trembling followers were clinging to the bulwarks, too shaken to speak. He got them together and promised he'd bring them to a safe harbour and would do his best to make life pleasant for them.

Beams cracked, doors sprang open. "This is the end!" McClure cried, "The ship is breaking up; in five minutes she will be sunk."

In fact, Robert McClure was a changed man. All the gambling spirit seemed to have been sucked out of him by this last encounter with the elements. Before many days had passed, the ship entered the main channel northeast of Banks Island that would later be named for McClure. Barrow Strait and Lancaster Sound, the continuation of the Passage, lay just ahead.

For most of September, the expedition moved to the southeast. The ship hugged the coast of Banks Island, a forbidding shore without a bay or a harbour that might offer shelter or protection; a journey, in Dr. Armstrong's words, that "should never be again attempted; and … I feel convinced … will never be made again."

But at last the *Investigator* reached a large bay. McClure named it Mercy Bay. Later the doctor remarked that some of the men thought it ought to have been called that because "it would have been a mercy had we never entered it." For the bay was a dead end. Here the crew would be confined for the next two years. The ship itself would never be able to leave.

Dr. Armstrong, who was always critical of McClure, thought that he should have gone on to Edward Parry's Winter Harbour, or even farther east to complete the transit of the Passage. It is more than possible he might have accomplished that feat. A few days later his sailing master found open water as far as the eye could see.

But McClure was taking no chances. What had happened to the daring captain who had once gambled on a fast shortcut through the Aleutians and a careless dash past the Arctic pack off Banks Island? Was it a failure of nerve as some would later say? Perhaps. But it must be remembered that he and his crew had come through a frightful experience. He had been lucky three times. And it was September 23, very late in the season.

For once, Robert McClure put the safety of his ship and ship's company ahead of his personal ambitions. He could not know that this latest decision would come close to being the death of them all.

It was not an easy winter for Robert McClure and his men. In his haste to find a secluded harbour, he had chosen a trap—and he soon realized it. Suspecting that the ice in that sheltered backwater might not melt the following summer, he reduced rations. The doctor insisted the diet wasn't enough to keep the crew healthy. By April 1852, the men were losing weight at an alarming rate. But McClure stuck to his quota. When three half-starved men stole some meat, he had them flogged.

CHAPTER FIVE

The Rescue

ONLY THREE SEARCH VESSELS REMAINED IN THE ARCTIC THAT WINTER OF
1851–52: MCCLURE IN THE *INVESTIGATOR* AT MERCY BAY; COLLINSON IN THE
ENTERPRISE, ANCHORED OFF VICTORIA ISLAND ON THE EASTERN SHORE OF
PRINCE OF WALES STRAIT; AND, FIVE HUNDRED MILES (800 KM) TO THE EAST IN
PRINCE REGENT INLET (JUST WEST OF BAFFIN ISLAND), THE LITTLE *PRINCE
ALBERT*, HIRED BY LADY FRANKLIN. EVERYONE ELSE HAD RETURNED TO
ENGLAND WHERE PRESS AND PUBLIC WERE DEMANDING THE NAVY TRY ONCE
MORE TO FIND FRANKLIN AND HIS MEN.

To this chorus was now added the voice of Lieutenant Cresswell's father,
who was also demanding that there be a separate search for the *Investigator*,
on which his son was serving. Nobody had heard a whisper of McClure and
his ship since August 1850.

In April 1852 a five-ship squadron under an aging commander, Sir
Edward Belcher, was ordered north to continue the search. That same
month, McClure set off on a search of his own.

Travelling by sledge across the rough ice of the strait later named for
him, he started for Parry's Winter Harbour on Melville Island—a journey
that he should have made the previous year. And there, on the summit of a
great sandstone block, he found a flat tin case containing a message for him.
To his dismay he saw that it had been left there the previous June.

Now, as he realized the depth of his negligence and the seriousness of
his position, Robert McClure sat down and wept like a child. The other
ships searching for Franklin, he realized, must have gone home. By now his
would-be rescuers were all back in England. Everything he had worked for,
the triumphs he had achieved, the charting of new lands as well as the
crowning discovery of them all—the Passage—were as dust. There was little hope of rescue; he would not live to bask in his success.

He got back to the ship in May. Scurvy was spreading through the crew. By July, sixteen men suffered from it. Dr. Armstrong was urging a better diet to help them regain their strength, but McClure, facing another winter in Mercy Bay, refused. Freshly killed muskoxen and a quantity of wild sorrel helped to stall the disease. It was not enough, however, to stop the hunger. One desperate man stole a loaf of bread knowing that punishment awaited. He got three dozen strokes of the cat-o'-nine-tails on his bare back.

McClure meant to stretch out his rations as long as he could. When August arrived it was clear that Mercy Bay would remain locked in the ice. It was shaped like a funnel—fifteen miles (24 km) deep and seven miles (11 km) broad at the entrance, where shoals caught the ice to form a barrier. The previous September this opening had been free of ice. But this season of 1852 was a slow one. By August 27 the young ice was strong enough to allow the crews to skate to the shore.

Now once again the land turned white. The men had nothing to do. One, Mark Bradbury, was clearly going mad. Although McClure kept up a cheerful attitude, Miertsching could hear him praying and sighing alone in his cabin.

On September 9 he got his crew together and told them what they already suspected—they were stuck for another winter. He tried to cheer them up, promising that they would all get home safely. But then he was forced to reveal that the half rations they had been living on for the past year would be cut back again.

They were down to one meal a day. Most ate their ration of half a pound (227 g) of salt meat raw because it shrank so much when it was cooked. A group got together and pleaded for more food. They said the men were so hungry they couldn't sleep. Again, McClure refused. And now another man, Sub-Lieutenant Robert Wynniatt, went mad from hunger. By the end of 1852, each man was thirty-five pounds (16 kg) lighter, and twenty were ill with scurvy.

As the winter dragged on, the health of the men grew worse. The two mental cases howled all night, contributing to the gloom. At one point Wynniatt tried to kill his captain. Another sailor, stiff with the cold, fell and broke his leg. By the end of January, one clerk, Joseph Paine, and one of the mates, Herbert Sainsbury, were close to death.

The ship, too, seemed to be suffering. The bolts and fastenings cracked in the sixty-degree-below-Fahrenheit (−51°C) cold. Miertsching noted that the doctor's reports had reduced McClure to despair. "How it must affect our captain," he wrote, "… when he sees his once-strong, rugged and hearty crew wasted away and scarcely with the strength to hold themselves upright."

The captain had concocted a dangerous plan the previous fall, and now, on March 2, prepared to put it into operation. He had decided that twenty of the strongest men would stay with the ship. Those who could not last another winter would try to get to civilization. One party would head for the depot and boat he had cached at Princess Royal Island on Prince of Wales Strait. With the food from that depot, they might be able to reach the mouth of the Mackenzie River. Another would travel to Port Leopold on the northeast corner of Somerset Island, where James Clark Ross had left a boatload of supplies. They would try to reach the whaling grounds in Baffin Bay.

It was a reckless, desperate scheme. In effect, McClure was sending the sick men to their deaths. As the doctor knew, there wasn't any hope that in their weakened condition they could survive such a lengthy and difficult journey. Sixteen were hospitalized. The demented Wynniatt couldn't be made to understand that he was to leave the ship. Bradbury, in the doctor's words, "must be handled like an idiot child."

Even healthy men would find it difficult to make those long journeys. But McClure felt he had to take some action. If the forty weakest men stayed, they would surely die with the others. There was just a slim chance that the twenty-two who remained might get through—for one thing there would be fewer men to divide the food.

The strange thing is that those detailed to leave were delighted at the prospect, while those who were chosen to stay with the ship were bitterly disappointed. Apparently McClure didn't realize that if by some miracle the ship was saved and he got back to England with the survivors, he would never be able to raise his head again in civilized company for having abandoned the sick.

On April 5, just as the sledges were ready to go, John Boyle, one of the men designated to leave, died of scurvy. McClure called all hands to the quarterdeck and delivered another of those eloquent morale-building addresses that seemed to rally them. He told them to be true to themselves and to the service, not to despair, but to look forward to the future with determination. In the gloomiest hour, he said, relief might easily come.

The next day he and Haswell were walking on the ice with Miertsching, discussing the problem of how to dig a grave for Boyle in ground that was frozen granite-solid.

"Sir," said McClure to the missionary, "if next year in Europe you neither see nor hear of me, then you may be sure that Captain McClure, along with his crew, has perished and lies unburied but wrapped in the fur coat which you gave me, enjoying a long and tranquil sleep until awakened on the Day of Resurrection by the Redeemer in Whom is all my hope and trust ..."

At that moment he was interrupted by one of his seamen, who rushed up to announce that something black was moving on the heavy ice near the sea. He thought it was a muskox, but it wasn't. A second seaman came running up.

"They are men," he cried. "First a man, then a sledge with men."

Apart from their shipmates, the seamen had not seen another human being for twenty-one months. Who were these? Inuit, perhaps? McClure and his companions held their breaths as one of the strangers drew nearer. The first man looked like a Native with a face "as black as old Nick."

"In the name of God," cried McClure, "who are you?"

The stranger stepped forward and uttered a sentence that ran through them all like an electric shock. "I am Lieutenant Pim, late of the *Herald*, now of the *Resolute* ..."

So the miracle that McClure had hoped for had come to pass. The relief he had promised his crew was at hand. Once again, in his darkest hour, Providence had smiled on Robert John Le Mesurier McClure.

CHAPTER SIX

A Cruel Decision

MCCLURE AND HIS MEN WERE SAVED BECAUSE THE BRITISH PUBLIC, PUSHED ON BY THE INDOMITABLE LADY FRANKLIN, HAD REFUSED TO LET THE ROYAL NAVY GIVE UP ON THE SEARCH.

In that spring of 1853, unknown to McClure, the five British naval vessels under the command of Sir Edward Belcher had taken up the task of finding the two lost expeditions. They were sent to look for Franklin, of course, but they were also looking for McClure and Collinson.

The previous September, one of the searchers, Leopold M'Clintock, had come upon McClure's letter written the previous April and left on the site of Parry's Winter Harbour. The letter told of the *Investigator* being caught in the ice of Mercy Bay. It was too late in the season that year to rescue McClure. That would have to wait until the spring of 1853. But as early as possible—earlier than any spring journey yet made by the Navy in the Arctic—a small expedition set off on the rescue attempt.

At this point, McClure had been out of touch with the outside world for two and a half years. He had no idea what was going on in the Arctic or elsewhere. His family had been unable to write him. The only letter he had dispatched had lain under the cairn at Parry's Winter Harbour for six months before it was discovered. Had Franklin been found? McClure had no way of knowing. Were there other vessels in the Arctic? Was anybody trying to find him? Like many Arctic explorers before him, McClure was totally in the dark.

The man who volunteered to find McClure was a remarkable young naval lieutenant, named Bedford Pim. He had been one of the last to see McClure before that expedition vanished into the western Arctic in the summer of 1850. Pim at that time was serving aboard the *Herald* under

Captain Henry Kellett—the same Captain Kellett who had tried to stop McClure from making his rash dash into the heart of the Arctic maze. Now Kellett was in charge of two ships anchored off Melville Island. It was he who sent Pim on his voyage of relief.

Pim was not a typical naval man. He was an individualist who had earlier made an ambitious plan to cross Siberia in search of Franklin. He wanted help from the Russians, but they had no money, and so, when he learned that Kellett was going north again, he volunteered to join him. Now, in March of 1853, he was sledging west across the frozen expanse of Melville Sound on a rescue mission.

McClure wanted to keep it all— and all the glory too. To do that he had to keep up the pretence that his men were healthy enough to sail the ship out of the Arctic and home to England.

It was typical of Pim that he took a small party of ten men with him—with one sledge only, and one small dogsled. When the man-hauled sledge broke down, Pim sent all but two of his party back and, always the loner, mushed on with his dogs. The temperature stood at fifty degrees below Fahrenheit (–46ºC). It was slow going. It took him twenty-eight days to reach the cliffs of Mercy Bay. He moved along the sullen coastline seeking a cairn, not knowing that McClure's ship was hidden from view by the hummocky ice. At last, one of his men pointed to a black spot on the bay. Pim got out his telescope, saw it was a ship, left his sled behind, and pushed forward, throwing his hat into the air and screeching into the wind.

A wild scene followed. When McClure finally identified his rescuer as a man he had last seen near Bering Strait—his face black with the soot of his coal-oil lamp—the news that he sent back to his ship was at first treated as a joke. Then came a celebration. The sick sprang from their beds. The tradesmen laid down their tools. All those who could crawl poured out of the hatchway. Some couldn't trust their eyes and began to touch and paw their rescuers.

Pim was shocked by their experience and even more shocked to learn that their next meal consisted only of a tiny piece of bread and a cup of weak cocoa. He sent back to his sledge for a package of bacon. His own men were so affected that tears rolled down their cheeks.

The next morning McClure got his crew together to remind them that he had urged them to trust the mysterious workings of the Almighty. And thus was averted a second Arctic tragedy, one that would have matched that of John Franklin. But the miseries of the *Investigator* party were not yet ended, for now the nasty side of McClure's character showed itself.

Kellett's man, Pim, had saved McClure. Thus it followed that Kellett and his crew were eligible for at least part of the prize of ten thousand pounds that Parliament had voted for the discovery of the North West Passage. McClure wanted to keep it all—and all the glory too. To do that he had to keep up the pretence that his men were healthy enough to sail the ship out of the Arctic and home to England, not helped by Kellett or anybody else. And so, he rushed off immediately to try to persuade Kellett that he was perfectly able to keep going.

In order to make the scheme believable, he left two instructions, both cruel. The twenty-four members of the crew who were desperately ill would leave on April 15 by sledge and make their way to Kellett's two vessels off Melville Island. The remainder were to stay with the ship and continue on the *same rations* that had brought them to a state of near starvation. This callous order was designed to show that the expedition didn't need any help.

By the time the party of sick set off, three more of the ship's company were dead. It was a ghastly journey—half of the men were so miserable and lame they couldn't stand upright. Their stronger comrades had to tend to their needs by day and even put them to bed at night. It was the spectacle of this scarecrow party of shrunken creatures, tottering forward, hollow-eyed, staring blankly ahead, which convinced Kellett that McClure couldn't carry on as he claimed he could.

Kellett now suggested McClure abandon his ship. But once again the wily McClure insisted he must obey his orders. He said he couldn't abandon the *Investigator* on his own responsibility. Kellett thought he was being noble. In fact, McClure was looking forward to a time when he would be able to swear with a straight face before an inquiry that he had been quite prepared to go on without help—in short, that he, and he alone, was the conqueror of the Passage.

Kellett suggested a compromise. McClure would go back to the ship with Dr. Armstrong, and, if the men were fit and willing, he would carry on.

Armstrong, of course, was one of his severest critics, so McClure suggested that one of Kellett's surgeons also accompany them. But when they reached the *Investigator* on May 19, McClure, to his surprise and dismay, found that only four men out of twenty would volunteer to go on. Both doctors agreed they shouldn't, and that was it. Kellett's order to abandon his ship was now in effect, and the *Investigator* was left to her fate.

Meanwhile, the search for John Franklin and his missing ships continued. Sledging parties under Leopold M'Clintock—who commanded Kellett's sister ship—fanned out to explore the western Arctic and search for Franklin in the unlikely event that he'd managed to get that far. Struggling in harness like so many beasts of burden, dragging back-breaking loads as heavy as 280 pounds (127 kg) a man, sometimes trudging knee-deep in slush, they performed superhuman feats at enormous personal cost.

Was it really necessary to send out big ten-man sledges loaded down with supplies when two or three dog drivers could cover the same ground? Nobody, apparently, bothered to consider that.

By the time the sledge crews got back, the surviving members of the *Investigator*'s company were lodged aboard Kellett's two vessels. It must have seemed to them that their troubles were over. For here there was plenty of game, including ten thousand pounds (4,500 kg) of muskox and caribou meat that had been taken that summer.

With no sign of Franklin in the western Arctic, Kellett's plan was to take his ships back to Beechey Island, which had become the headquarters of the British search expedition. He set off when the ice broke on August 18, to the great joy of the men of the *Investigator*. Two transport ships, accompanied by a steamer, *Phoenix*, were due to arrive from England with supplies and mail. Then they would return and the men would be homeward-bound at last! It seemed to be too good to be true—and it was.

They reckoned without the Arctic weather. Kellett's two ships had scarcely moved more than a hundred miles (160 km) to the east before the ice closed in again. Now, McClure's men, who had suffered through three dreadful Arctic winters, faced a fourth.

A few got away because McClure wanted to get the news of his discovery to England. He had already sent Cresswell to Beechey Island by sledge with the demented Wynniatt. There they met the steamer, *Phoenix*, carrying letters and dispatches from home. Her steam power had allowed her to break through the ice pack and open up a passage for the transport ships that brought the new supplies for the depot. In spite of this, one of the transports, *Breadalbane*, was crushed in the ice and sank in fifteen minutes, though her crew was rescued. More than a century later, in 1981, Canadian divers found her in 340 feet (104 m) of water.

At the end of August, the *Phoenix* managed to nose through the ice pack and get to England with Cresswell and his news. The discovery of the North West Passage was "a triumph not for this age alone but for mankind," in the words of Lord Stanley, the secretary of state for the colonies. Cresswell was reunited with his father, to whom, as much as to anyone, he owed his life.

And so the news was out: McClure had been found and he, himself, had found the North West Passage, though he had not been able to navigate it. No one had yet made it all the way through from one ocean to another, and no one would until Roald Amundsen managed the feat in a long trip that started in 1903 and ended in 1906—half a century after McClure's first discovery.

CHAPTER SEVEN

The High Cost of Dawdling

MCCLURE HAD BEEN FOUND. BUT WHERE WAS COLLINSON, HIS SUPERIOR OFFI-
CER? THE TWO WERE SUPPOSED TO HAVE STUCK TOGETHER, BUT THE RASH AND
AMBITIOUS MCCLURE HAD RUSHED ON AHEAD AND MADE HIS DISCOVERY, LEAV-
ING COLLINSON FAR IN THE REAR.

In fact, Collinson was doomed to spend five winters away from home,
and to be out of touch with the civilized world for three years. He was more
prudent than McClure. He took no gambles and so he was cheated of the
ultimate prize.

He had one other problem: he could not speak the native language
because his interpreter, Johann Miertsching, the Moravian missionary, was
not with him. Miertsching was supposed to have transferred from
McClure's ship to Collinson's in Honolulu in the summer of 1850. But, as
we have seen, Collinson left before he arrived. The result was that, even if
Collinson had encountered Natives who had some clue to Franklin's fate, he
would not have been able to talk to them.

Collinson's ship was not a happy one. Problems began when he cau-
tiously took the longer route to Bering Strait. The winds weren't as bad in
the Aleutians as he had been told—and as the more daring McClure discovered. But even before he reached the Bering Sea in mid-August,
Collinson seemed frightened of wintering in the Arctic and was already
talking of going back to Hong Kong.

He had made a serious error in sailing around the northern coast of
Russian Alaska. He believed the coastal waters were so shallow that it would
be dangerous to get within fifteen miles (24 km) of the mainland. As it
turned out, he was wrong. There was plenty of depth nearer the shore.

The permanent Arctic ice pack fifteen miles (24 km) from the coast posed a more serious threat. Collinson reached Point Barrow at the northwest tip of Alaska—but wouldn't go nearer than twenty-five miles (40 km) offshore. Then he turned back. He was convinced that an Open Polar Sea lay to the northwest. But there was no Open Polar Sea, despite the belief of many mariners. From that point on, there was only solid ice.

His ice master, Francis Skead, wrote that "this cursed *polar basin* ... is one of the phantoms which has led to our failure." If it hadn't held them back, they might have found an open channel along the coastline. "We now end the season to continue to seek for what no one but the Captain believes has any existence." They were eighteen days behind McClure.

The *Enterprise* returned the way it had come, and rounded the northwest corner of Alaska, heading south. On August 30 at Point Hope, south of Cape Lisburne, Collinson found what he had missed on the northern journey—a note in a cairn from Kellett reporting that McClure was ahead of him. He was astounded and angry. If only he had found the message earlier! Then he would have certainly pressed on and caught up with McClure. Still, there was time to catch up—or so his officers believed.

"For God's sake, go back at once, it is not now too late," the surgeon, Robert Anderson, pleaded.

"No, no!" Collinson replied, "I must seek Kellett."

Kellett was farther south at Grantley Harbour at this time in his ship, *Herald.* So was Thomas Moore in the supply ship *Plover.* Collinson reached them on September 1. According to Skead, Moore told him there was a good anchorage in a harbour off Point Barrow, and Kellett urged him to retrace his steps.

"If you make haste, Coll, you'll be able to winter at Point Barrow."

"No, no," said Collinson. "I'm not going to take *my* ship there."

Instead he dawdled, deciding to seek winter quarters somewhere on the northwest coast of Alaska. Two weeks dragged by before he decided to go north again. He got as far as Icy Cape on September 22, but finding no suitable harbour, he stopped. One of his officers offered to go on to Point Barrow alone to check the harbour there. Collinson refused, turned south again, and spent the winter at Hong Kong.

This was a costly decision. When he got back the following July, and once again rounded the Alaskan peninsula, it became painfully clear that, had he kept on and wintered at Point Barrow, he would almost certainly have caught up with McClure. Then the two of them would have shared the honour of discovering a North West Passage.

Now Collinson got himself trapped in the ice pack off Point Barrow. It turned out there was a lane of open water and none of the shoals he had feared. He tried to make for that open lane, but was helplessly pushed back westward. By this time his ice master, Skead, whom he had ignored, was scarcely on speaking terms with him. Skead was impatient to move ahead, especially as the sea was calm by August 12. But instead of putting his men to work hauling the ship through the lanes in the melting ice, Collinson insisted on waiting for the wind to improve.

In that short season every mile counted. Yet there was no sense of urgency aboard the Enterprise.

In that short season every mile counted. Yet there was no sense of urgency aboard the *Enterprise*. An ordinary yachtsman might have taken his craft east, Skead thought—"aye & his wife and daughters to boot." He had never seen men have it so easy aboard any ship on which he'd served. "As we make so little progress when there are so few obstacles to our advance, I am afraid to think of what we shall do if we meet with difficulty from ice. Poor Sir John! God help you—you'll get none from us."

Collinson finally reached the southern tip of Banks Island on August 26, 1851, and took possession of it in the name of the Queen. He couldn't know that McClure had been there the year before and already named it Nelson Head. The following day, at the Princess Royal Islands, they discovered that McClure had also been there—just six weeks before.

They sailed up Prince of Wales Strait—again not knowing that McClure had been ahead of them—and were stopped by the ice as McClure had been. Turning back, they rounded Banks Island from the east, and there, once again, found that McClure had been on the ground before them. In fact, at this moment he was only two weeks in the lead.

If Collinson had gone ahead, he could easily have wintered with the *Investigator* at Mercy Bay and taken charge of the combined expedition. But again he turned back, and on September 13 went into winter quarters on the eastern coast of Prince of Wales Strait at Walker Bay. This was then known as Prince Albert Land, but it is actually part of the massive Victoria Island, as Collinson himself was to discover. Once again, Collinson found that others had been there before him—the sledge crew of Lieutenant Haswell of the *Investigator*.

The weather remained fine. Five weeks went by before the ocean began to ice up. Collinson could have found a wintering harbour farther south and put himself in a better position for a thrust to the east the next spring. But he didn't.

His ice master was beside himself with frustration. "How much we have lost, it is painful to contemplate," he noted. His captain's inactivity was "a marvellous proceeding considering Franklin was perishing for food and shelter." Collinson's relations with Skead were so strained that by April 1852 the ice master was put under permanent arrest.

The *Enterprise* left winter quarters that summer, and squeezed through Dolphin and Union Strait (south of Victoria Island) and through the island maze of Coronation Gulf—a remarkable feat of navigation on Collinson's part. But again, Collinson, without knowing it, was covering ground already explored by the men of the Hudson's Bay Company in the Franklin search.

The expedition wintered at Cambridge Bay on the southeastern shore of Victoria Island, no more than 120 miles (193 km) from King William Island, which had not yet been explored. That, in fact, was where the clues to the loss of the Franklin expedition were to be found—for that is where the survivors had died.

Thus, Collinson could have solved the mystery of both the North West Passage and the fate of the lost explorer. Once again he muffed it. When he tried to question the Natives who visited the ship that winter of 1852-53, he had nobody to translate. Almost certainly the Inuit had tales to tell of sinking ships and dying men only a few-score miles to the east. One of his officers, in fact, got some of the Natives to draw a map of the coastline to the east. He thought the Inuit artists were indicating ships in that area. Collinson would have none of it.

In April 1853, Collinson led a sledging party up the west coast of Victoria Strait, and there he discovered a note in a cairn that told him that John Rae of the Hudson's Bay Company had covered the same ground two years before! Once again he had lost out on his discovery.

If he had only known earlier, he could have crossed Victoria Strait to

King William Land and found the secret of the missing expedition. Victory Point, where the clues to the mystery lay hidden in a cairn of rocks, was less than forty miles (64 km) away. But Collinson, always cautious, worried about the roughness of the ice, and so the opportunity passed him by.

The frustrated Skead thought the whole area could and should have been investigated. "Two serving officers in good health & strong were under arrest on trifling charges," he wrote, adding that there were plenty of men available also to explore the estuary of the Great Fish River. But Collinson wasn't listening to Skead.

In July one of his crew members came upon some wreckage not far from Cambridge Bay. This included a fragment of a door frame that almost certainly came from one of Franklin's ships. Collinson missed its significance. His fuel was running low, and so he turned west again to winter at Camden Bay on the north coast of Alaska.

When the *Enterprise* finally reached Port Clarence on the west coast of the Alaskan peninsula on August 24, 1854, the officers of the British supply ship *Rattlesnake* were shocked at the state of discipline that existed on board. At that point every one of Collinson's executive officers was under arrest. None had been allowed off the ship for fifteen months. Skead had been confined for two years and eight months.

When Collinson finally returned to England in May 1855, he had managed to visit and explore all the mysterious "lands" that might or might not have been islands—Banks, Baring, Wollaston, and Victoria. He had sailed up Prince of Wales Strait, and had got as far as Victoria Strait directly across from King William Island, and yet his voyage was a failure because he discovered nothing new. Wherever he went he found others had gone before him.

Had he been a year or two earlier, he might have emerged as one of the greatest of the Arctic explorers. As it was, he returned to England with the reputation of a man who had simply covered old ground. His reception was chilly, not because of his failures, but because he was in trouble with his own officers. At one time or another they had all been under arrest. Now he demanded that they all be court-martialled, but the British Admiralty would have none of that. It was understandable that, after four years cooped up on a crowded ship, even disciplined men would feel the tension.

The embattled captain had only one claim to fame. He had shown that the narrow passage along the North American coastline could actually be navigated by a large ship. Until that point, it had not been believed possible. And that was the passage that Roald Amundsen eventually followed. In short, there was more than one North West Passage. There were in fact three.

Collinson emerged from his long Arctic confinement a bitter man. He was angry because the Navy refused to court-martial his officers. He was even more angry when the committee investigating claims to the discovery of the Passage passed him by.

Robert McClure and his crew got ten thousand pounds for their discovery. Collinson got nothing more than an honourable mention. Richard Collinson was so upset with the Admiralty that he never again applied for a naval command. Nor did anybody rush to offer him one.

As for Robert McClure, he, too, faced moments of anticlimax. In spite of the rewards and honour heaped upon him, there was still a suspicion that Franklin had discovered a North West Passage before McClure. And that later turned out to be true. In 1859 Leopold M'Clintock, working for Lady Franklin, discovered the relics of her husband's lost expedition on King William Island. As a result, the missing explorer was credited with being the first to discover a North West Passage, making it clear that no single channel ran through the Arctic islands.

Whether or not Franklin had actually seen the Passage as it led through Victoria Strait in Queen Maud Gulf could never be known. But he had got close enough to it to make it likely, and sentiment was on his side, thanks to his widow's determined efforts to memorialize his name.

And so this sentimental decision downgraded McClure's later discovery of another passage farther north. Unlike Franklin, McClure had actually traversed the Passage from east to west, though not entirely by water. But Franklin was a popular favourite. McClure's naked ambition had given him a brief moment of glory, but, in the end, it reduced him to the second rank of polar explorers. Nonetheless, he prospered. Knighted by the Queen, Sir Robert was posted to the China seas and ended his days as a vice-admiral.

The story of the search for the North West Passage is made up of tales—tales like McClure's—of disappointment, frustration, of naked ambition, and also of daring, courage, and resourcefulness. The rash Robert McClure and his more cautious commander, Collinson, are part of that story. Both their sagas are tied to the search for Franklin and the search for the North West Passage. But as in so many other cases, it was the search itself that counted, not the goal. Their real contribution was to open up the mysterious, frozen Arctic world—a world of treeless, windswept islands, some vast, some tiny, which we know now as the Arctic Archipelago.

This archipelago is part of Canada today because of men like McClure, Collinson, Pim, and Kellett—and John Franklin himself.

INDEX

About Fifth House

Fifth House Publishers, a Fitzhenry & Whiteside company, is a proudly western-Canadian press. Our publishing specialty is non-fiction as we believe that every community must possess a positive understanding of its worth and place if it is to remain vital and progressive. Fifth House is committed to "bringing the West to the rest" by publishing approximately twenty books a year about the land and people who make this region unique. Our books are selected for their quality, and contribution to the understanding of western-Canadian (and Canadian) history, culture, and environment.

Look for the following Fifth House titles at your local bookstore:

Canada Moves West,
    Pierre Berton
The Golden Trail: The Story of the Klondike Rush,
    Pierre Berton
Homemade Fun: Games & Pastimes of the Early Prairies,
    Faye Reineberg Holt
Monarchs of the Fields: The Story of the Combine Harvester,
    Faye Reineberg Holt
The Nor'Westers: The Fight for the Fur Trade,
    Marjorie Wilkins Campbell
Prairie Sentinel: The Story of the Canadian Grain Elevator,
    Brock V. Silversides
The Savage River: Seventy-one Days with Simon Fraser,
    Marjorie Wilkins Campbell
Settling In: First Homes on the Prairies,
    Faye Reineberg Holt
Threshing: The Early Years of Harvesting,
    Faye Reineberg Holt

Pierre Berton's History for Young Canadians

"The stories are so real that it's as though Berton is leading us down the surveyor's mountain paths, helping us swing the hammer on the rails, or cut the sod along with the pioneers. Canadian history is alive and well, thanks in large part to Pierre Berton." –from the Foreword by Arthur Slade, author of *Dust* and the *Canadian Chills* series.

The first book in Fifth House's *Pierre Berton's History for Young Canadians* series is *Canada Moves West*, a rousing collection of five young-adult, non-fiction books by revered author Pierre Berton. These books describe how, back in the days of the pioneers, the Canadian west was won—with blood, sweat, tears, and sheer determination.

Originally printed as separate volumes in the *Adventures in Canadian History* series, the titles in *Canada Moves West* include:

The Railway Pathfinders
The Men in Sheepskin Coats
A Prairie Nightmare
Steel Across the Plains
Steel Across the Shield

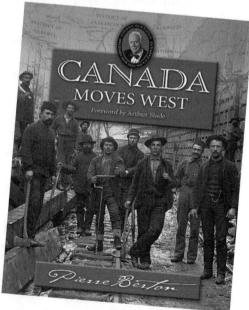

Riveting history abounds in the books. Find out about:

🍁 The romantic and gritty adventures of railway pathfinders such as the indomitable Walter Moberly, and railway builders, Joseph Whitehead and Harry Armstrong, who fought their way from the gnarled rocks of the Canadian Shield to the passes of three mountain ranges in British Columbia

* The epic tales of the immigrants in sheepskin coats from Eastern Europe, who braved hardship and discrimination to create new lives in a new land, successfully settling the wide open spaces of the Canadian prairies

* The story of those whose lives were forever changed by the coming of the railway: the Cree and Blackfoot peoples, led by Chiefs Piapot, Big Bear, and Crowfoot

COMING SOON—the third book in the *Pierre Berton's History for Young Canadians* series: The *Battles of the War of 1812*, a seven-book collection that captures the history and the characters who made that history during the great battles of this war.

Originally a part of the *Adventures in Canadian History* series, titles in *The Battles of the War of 1812* include:

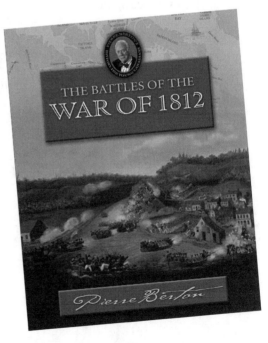

The Capture of Detroit
The Death of Isaac Brock
Revenge of the Tribes
Canada Under Siege
The Battle of Lake Erie
The Death of Tecumseh
Attack on Montreal

In this series, Berton continues to use the techniques that made him one of Canada's best storytellers, recreating the dramatic scenes from a war that would shape the new Canada and define the Canadian character.

Read all about:

- John Richardson, the curly-haired, fifteen-year-old "gentleman" volunteer who rushed to serve his country in June of 1812
- The brave General Isaac Brock, a man now made into a myth, who died defending Upper Canada at the Battle of Queenston Heights
- The commander of the British fleet, Robert Heriot Barclay (whose nine sailing ships were built from timber from the forests around Lake Erie), and the Battle of Lake Erie, the only battle ever to be fought on a Canadian lake
- The great Shawnee leader Tecumseh, who dreamt of forming a strong alliance of tribes that would be able to protect Native lands from American troops and settlers
- The incredible story of how only a few hundred men managed to fight off the tired and ill-equipped Americans at the Battle of Châteauguay

AND, WATCH FOR—the fourth book in this exciting

Canadian history series, *The Great Klondike Gold Rush*, including:

Bonanza Gold
The Klondike Stampede
Trails of '89
City of Gold, Kings of the Klondike
Before the Gold Rush